A NEW APPROACH
TO LATIN FOR THE MASS

ASSOCIATION FOR LATIN LITURGY

A NEW APPROACH TO LATIN FOR THE MASS

by

LOUISE RILEY-SMITH

and

CHRISTOPHER FRANCIS

Illustrations by
JOHN RYAN
with a foreword by
His Eminence BASIL, CARDINAL HUME O.S.B.

ASSOCIATION FOR LATIN LITURGY

First published 1987

© 1987 Association for Latin Liturgy

Second edition reprinted with corrections 2000
Reprinted 2006

ISBN-10: 0 9504498 5 7
ISBN-13: 978 0 9504498 5 2

Some of John Ryan's cartoons included in this book first appeared in slightly
different forms in the *Catholic Herald*

Origination and typesetting by Association for Latin Liturgy
47 Western Park Road, Leicester, LE3 6HQ

Printed in England by The Lavenham Press, Lavenham, Suffolk

FOREWORD BY CARDINAL HUME

The use of modern languages in the liturgy is one of the main changes in the practice of the Church in the past twenty years. Most of the faithful have unquestionably found it profitable to understanding and devotion. It is nevertheless important that we should not lose sight of the richness of Latin liturgical celebration, the sense of continuity with Christians in past ages and unity with those of the present which it affords, and its association with our heritage of Church music of every period up to and including our own.

Many students for the priesthood and many of the laity whose reverence and sense of the sacred would be enhanced by a knowledge of the universal language of the Church have had no opportunity of acquiring it. Others may have lost their familiarity with it through lack of practice. This book is designed to present to all the essentials of the Latin of the Mass of the new Western rite, and I warmly commend it.

ARCHBISHOP'S HOUSE, WESTMINSTER
FEAST OF ALL SAINTS 1986

INTRODUCTION

This book is intended primarily for priests and those studying for the priesthood, who wish to celebrate Mass in Latin with full understanding. We hope that the laity also will find it useful.

It is essentially a method of learning by doing; at every stage we have included exercises, to which answers are provided.

All the vocabulary and grammar are introduced with the Latin Mass of the new rite in mind: the full texts, with official translations, may be found in the *Missal,* also published by the Association for Latin Liturgy.

Although Mass is celebrated in the modern vernacular throughout the Western Church, Latin continues to prove its vitality and its special value. Indeed it is the intention of the Church that the use of the Latin language is to be preserved in her liturgical rites. Its use is a reminder of the interior unity of the mind of Christ's mystical body. The concise nature of the Latin language enables the meaning of the liturgical texts to be retained; moreover, Latin contains nuances of meaning sometimes lost in the vernacular. Quite apart from its importance in Gregorian chant and other sacred music, Latin in the Liturgy is valuable as a language dedicated to the worship of God. The idea of a sacred language is an ancient one: it helps to convey a sense of the holy, which is under such threat today.

We all need roots, and the use of the Latin language links us with our fellow Christians down the ages. Just as it breaks through national barriers in the present, so it joins us to Christians in the past. It reinforces the depth and breadth of vision that have always been characteristic of the Catholic Church.

C.F., L.R.-S.

NOTE TO USERS OF THIS BOOK

This book is designed to save you as much time as possible. Everything in it is relevant to learning enough to celebrate Mass in Latin. Examples and exercises are taken almost entirely from the Liturgy. The vocabulary gives the meaning of all the words used in this book.

If you are working without the help of a teacher, make a resolution not to look at the answers until you have completed each exercise. Where there is a difference, try to see why our version differs from yours. Space is provided below each question for you to write your answer.

Many liturgical books use the letter 'i' for 'j': we have kept the distinction between 'i' and 'j' because we think this is helpful to the beginner.

A CD, *Orate Fratres*, is available to accompany this book. This has the Mass of the Holy Eucharist said in Latin with the Roman Canon, and also includes most of the priest's sung parts, and the most common sung responses.

Many recordings of Gregorian Chant are readily available, notably those made by the Benedictine monks of Solesmes.

STRUCTURE OF THIS BOOK

(a detailed plan of the sections of this book will be found on p xxiii)

'DOING WORDS' (verbs) in the prayer of the Missal

The prayer of the Missal is made up of:

1. Excerpts from the Scriptures.
2. Prayer composed by the Church.

In both prayer and quotation you will notice that four sorts of verbs occur:

A. STATEMENT. God *does* things, *will do* them, *has done* them.
Propter nos hómines, *descéndit* de caelis.
For us men, *he came down* from heaven.

B. PETITION. We ask God (or tell him like children!) to do things.

Da.	Concéde.	Fac.	Inténde.
Give.	Grant.	Do.	Listen.

C. WISH. We ask in a less direct tone, by wishing that something might happen.
Advéniat regnum tuum.
May your kingdom *come.*

D. WHY, WHEN and WHERE. We tag all sorts of extra ideas onto the main one: we say why, when or where something happened; we say what the purpose of our prayer is.

... *cum* amicítiam tuam *amisísset* ...
... *when he had lost* your friendship ...

... *ut* a peccáto *simus* semper líberi ...
... *so that we may* always *be* free from sin ...

It is of the utmost importance to be aware of what mood the action word is in. The book is divided into four sections arranged around these four central moods: they are the bare bones – the rest is the flesh that covers them.

'But I can't find the verb!'

THE ENGLISH LANGUAGE

We will examine: A) **Words** — what the different categories are, and how and why words change their endings;
                          B) **Sentences** — how these words are put together to convey meaning.

A)   WORDS

NOUNS name people and places, and things both perceptible to the senses and imperceptible.

1. **Common Nouns** are general terms for people and things: priest, altar, wine.
2. **Proper Nouns** name specific people, places, days: Saint Peter, Rome, Easter Sunday.
3. **Abstract Nouns** name concepts which the five senses cannot reach — qualities, feelings and ideas: holiness, contrition, unity.
4. **Collective Nouns** name a group of similar things or people: **congregation** of the faithful, **chorus** of angels.

PRONOUNS are words used to replace nouns: he, they, we, it, his, theirs.
Note especially **relative** pronouns which replace nouns or other pronouns so as to LINK them to a descriptive clause: This is the Lamb of God **who** takes away the sins of the world.

ADJECTIVES are words which describe nouns or pronouns: the **holy, catholic** Church. Note especially the degree or extent of adjectives: —comparative: holier, more holy.
superlative: holiest, very holy, most holy.
The English articles 'a' and 'the' are adjectives: they describe the noun as general or particular. There are **no** articles in Latin.

VERBS are words which   express an action or state — they are 'doing' or 'being' words: He **gave** thanks.
                                 Heaven and earth **are** full of your glory.

NOTE the following points about verbs:

1. The **Infinitive** is the form of a verb not governed or limited by person or number: it gives the **meaning** of the verb: to praise, to pray.
The infinitive is often needed to complete the sense of another verb: we hope **to enjoy** for ever the vision of your glory.
2. A **finite verb** is governed by a person: i.e. there is someone doing the action — I **confess** to Almighty God...
3. It has different **tenses** — expressing what is happening at the present moment, or what will happen in the future, or has happened in the past: Christ **has died,** Christ **is risen,** Christ **will come** again.
4. It expresses what the subject is doing or having done to him, i.e. is **Active** or **Passive**: on the third day **he rose** again. For our sake he **was crucified.**
5. It may express:
    i)   **a fact:** He **broke** the bread.
    ii) **a question:** Who **is** God but the Lord?
    iii) **a command: Do** this in memory of Me.
    iv) **a request** or **entreaty: Show** us, Lord, your mercy.
    v) **a wish** or **desire: May** the Lord **accept** the sacrifice at your hands.
    vi) **a possibility: If you,** O Lord, **should mark** our guilt, Lord, who **would survive?**

ADVERBS modify (tell us more about) verbs. They tell us more about the action in different ways:

1. **How:** a death he **freely** accepted.
2. **When** and **where: always** and **everywhere** we give you thanks.
3. **Why:** and **therefore** we join the angels and saints in proclaiming.
4. **How much:** I have sinned **too much.**

PREPOSITIONS are placed in front of nouns and pronouns to show the relation of these words to others in the sentence: **Through** him, **with** him, **in** him . . .; pray **for** me **to** the Lord.

CONJUNCTIONS are words which join words, phrases, clauses or sentences: heaven **and** earth are full of your glory; we proclaim your death ... **until** you come in glory; forgive us our trespasses **as** we forgive those ...

In the following sentences, each word has been identified:

I	—	pronoun
believe	—	verb
in	—	preposition
one	—	adjective
God	—	proper noun
the	—	adjective (article)
Father	—	proper noun
almighty	—	adjective

Exercise A

Identify each word or group of words in these sentences:

1. Father, you are holy indeed, and all creation rightly gives you praise.

2. You gather a people ... so that from East to West a perfect offering may be made.

3. Lord, by your cross and resurrection you have set us free.

4. I leave you peace, my peace I give you.

5. Those who hope in you shall not* be disappointed.

* *not* is an adverb

B) SENTENCES

A sentence is a collection of words, containing a finite verb which conveys a complete meaning. There are three kinds of sentence:

1. Simple
2. Compound
3. Complex

1. A **simple sentence** is made up of a **subject** – person or thing doing or receiving the action; and a **predicate** – statement of what he is doing (or receiving) and to what, how, where, etc.: Jesus broke the bread – **Jesus : subject, broke the bread :** predicate.

In the following sentence a circle has been put round the **subject** and the **predicate** has been underlined:

(He) **ascended into heaven.**

Exercise B

Circle the subject and underline the predicate in these sentences:

1. I am the true vine.

2. You teach us how to live in this passing world.

3. He proclaimed the good news of salvation.

4. The wise men followed the star.

5. With shouts of joy God goes up.

Simple sentences not only make **statements,** they may also make **petitions** and **commands** : Father, accept this offering from your whole family. Take this, all of you, and eat it.
They may also express **wishes** and **exhortations** : The Lord be with you. Let us call to mind our sins.

2. A **compound** sentence is made up of two or more simple ones joined by a conjunction: He put an end to death **and** revealed the resurrection.

3. A **complex** sentence is made of a simple one on which another (a 'subordinate clause') is dependent: This is the Lamb of God, **who takes away the sins of the world ...**

The easiest way of telling which is a subordinate part, is to ask: "Does it make sense on its own?"
e.g. 'This is the Lamb of God' is a complete sentence and makes sense on its own; 'who takes away the sins of the world' makes no sense on its own; we may see it as an extra part which belongs to the sentence.

Here are some other kinds of subordinate clauses:
Before he was given up to death ... he took bread . . .
Pray ... **that your sacrifice and mine may be acceptable to God** . . .
We praise you ... in this Easter season, **when Christ became our paschal sacrifice.**

Exercise C

Practise underlining the **subordinate clauses** in the following sentences:

1. I believe in the Holy Spirit ... who proceeds from the Father and the Son.

2. Protect us from all anxiety ... as we wait in joyful hope for the coming of our Saviour.

3. That we might live no longer for ourselves, he sent the Holy Spirit.

4. We do well to give you thanks, because you alone are God, living and true.

5. Sing a new song to the Lord, for he has worked wonders.

INFLECTION

> OBSTRUCT~~ING~~ THE DOORS CAUSE~~S~~
> DELAY AND ~~CAN~~ BE DANGEROUS!

The **meaning** of this notice, written above the doors of a tube train, was entirely altered: the **ENDINGS** of the words were **changed** (and a third scratched out).

The change in the **form** or **ending** of a word can change the **meaning** of:
1. a verb: he takes — he **took**
                                    I pray — l pray**ed**
                              You give — you g**ave**

2. a noun: angel — angel**s**
                              mouse — m**ice**
                                  lion — lion**ess**

3. pronouns: I — **me**
                               he — h**im**
                               she — **her**
                            they — the**m**
                          who — who**m**

You can see that the **verb** changed **tense**, the **noun** changed a) number (singular became plural) or b) gender: all **Latin** nouns are either masculine, feminine or neuter; the **pronoun** changed its 'case' (subject became object).

This change of the shape and endings of words is called **inflection.** English has comparatively little inflection; Latin has a lot, and uses it to express every shade of meaning.

Exercise D

1. Put these into the **plural:**

he is; I pray; she goes; heart; brother; sinner.

2. Put these into the **past tense:**

I confess; we believe; they become.

3. Change the case of these from **subject** to **object:**

I; we; who.

More about Cases

In English, **pronouns** show a change of case. **Nouns** do not; we use **prepositions** and the order of the words to show this. For example, we express the **possessive** case by using **of** before the noun or **'s** after it: 'the body **of** the Lord; the Lord**'s** body'. And we express the **nominative,** the subject case, by the order of the words: '**The wise men** followed the star' as distinct from 'the star followed the wise men'.

The **cases** are as follows:
1. **nominative** – names the subject of the sentence.
2. **vocative** – used to address people
3. **accusative** – the direct object of the sentence.
4. **genitive** – possessive case, showing ownership.
5. **dative** – expresses 'to' or 'for', indirect object.
6. **ablative** – expresses 'by', 'with' or 'from'.

Exercise E

Practise identifying the **case** of the nouns printed in bold in the following exercise.

1. **Christ** has died.

2. **Father,** accept this offering.

3. You have created all **things.**

4. With all the angels **of heaven** we sing …

5. He gave the cup **to** his **disciples.**

6. Through him, **with him,** in him …

BRIEF GUIDE TO PRONUNCIATION

1.   The most important thing in pronouncing Liturgical Latin is placing the main stress on the correct syllable. In words of two syllables this is always the first:

> **De**us
> **Chri**stus
> **Terra**

In words of three or more syllables the stressed syllable is marked in most liturgical books, and in this book, by a mark like the acute accent in French: é. On that syllable the voice rises slightly:

> Maríam
> **án**gelus
> ho**mí**nibus
> vol**tá**tis
> provi**dén**tia
> exsultati**ó**ne

As to the sounds of the letters, the pronunciation of Liturgical Latin is in many ways similar to modern Italian.

2.   Consonants:
> B, D, F, K, M, N, P, Q, V, X, Z
> are always pronounced exactly as in English:
> > **b**onus
> > **D**óminus
> > **pr**ovi**d**ebit etc.

> R and L are also pronounced as in English, but double R and double L need a distinct articulation of the second letter:
> > bella = bel-la
> > terra = ter-ra

> S is pronounced Z when single in the middle of a word:
> > mi**s**it
otherwise as SS:
> > Sanctus Dóminus; mi**ss**a

> C is pronounced K (**k**eep) before **a, o** and **u:**
> > **c**aput
> > **c**orpus
> > **c**um

and as Ch (**ch**urch) before **ae, e** and **i:**
> > **c**aeli
> > **c**essant
> > **c**ibum

> G behaves in the same way, hard (**g**o) before **a, o** and **u:**
> > **g**audent
> > a**g**o
> > lan**g**uóres

and soft (**g**em) before **e** and **i:**
> > án**g**elus
> > á**g**imus

> H is silent when it is the first letter of a word:
> > (h)omínibus
> > (h)osánna
otherwise as in English.

> J is always pronounced **i:**
> > **J**esus ‒ **I**esus
> > **J**erúsalem = **I**erúsalem

> T is hard (**t**ent) except before **-ia, -ie, -io** and **-iu,** when it is soft (tsi):
> > pa**ti**éntia = pa-tsien-tsia
> resurrec**ti**ónem = resurrects-ionem
> > pro**ti**us = propits-ius

> TH is always pronounced hard like t:
> > ca**th**ólicam = cattolicam

> W and Y do not exist in Latin.

3. Vowels in Latin are either long or short:

A
long: **a**ve as in f**a**ther
short: Mar**í**a as in h**a**ve

E
long: J**e**sus as in pr**ay**
short: **e**t as in h**e**n

I
long: bened**i**cat as in m**ee**t
short: **i**ncarnatus as in b**i**t

O
long: cred**o** as in h**o**me
short: D**o**minus as in h**o**t

U
long: loc**u**tus as in m**oo**n
short: sanct**u**s as in g**oo**d

AE, caeli, is always as in **ai**m.

'Non credo!'

Let us start by looking at the most familiar parts of the Ordinary of the Mass in Latin with an interlinear word-for-word English translation.

GLORIA   IN EXCELSIS   DEO,   ET IN   TERRA   PAX   HOMINIBUS   BONAE
Glory   in (the) highest   to God,   and in (on)   earth   peace   to men   of good

VOLUNTATIS.   LAUDAMUS   TE,   BENEDICIMUS   TE,   ADORAMUS   TE,
(of) will.   We praise   you,   we bless   you,   we adore   you,

GLORIFICAMUS   TE.   GRATIAS   AGIMUS   TIBI   PROPTER   MAGNAM   GLORIAM
we glorify   you.   Thanks   we give   to you   on account of   great   glory

TUAM: DOMINE   DEUS,   REX   CAELESTIS,   DEUS   PATER   OMNIPOTENS.
your: O Lord   God,   King   heavenly,   God   Father   all-powerful.

DOMINE   FILI   UNIGENITE,   JESU   CHRISTE: DOMINE   DEUS,   AGNUS
O Lord   Son   only-begotten   Jesus   Christ: O Lord   God,   Lamb

DEI,   FILIUS   PATRIS: QUI   TOLLIS   PECCATA   MUNDI,   MISERERE
of God,   Son   of the Father: who   take away   the sins   of the world,   have mercy

NOBIS: QUI TOLLIS   PECCATA   MUNDI,   SUSCIPE   DEPRECATIONEM   NOSTRAM;
on us;   who takes away   the sins   of the world,   receive   prayer   our;

QUI   SEDES   AD   DEXTERAM   PATRIS,   MISERERE   NOBIS.   QUONIAM
who   sits   at   the right (hand)   of the Father,   have mercy   on us.   Because

TU   SOLUS   SANCTUS,   TU   SOLUS   DOMINUS,   TU   SOLUS   ALTISSIMUS,
you (are)   alone   holy,   you (are)   alone   the Lord,   you (are)   alone   most high,

JESU   CHRISTE,   CUM   SANCTO   SPIRITU: IN   GLORIA   DEI   PATRIS.
Jesus   Christ,   with   Holy   (the) Spirit: in   glory   of God   (of) the Father.

AMEN.
Amen*

*__Amen__ *is a Hebrew word: it means 'so be it'.*

CREDO	IN	UNUM	DEUM,	PATREM	OMNIPOTENTEM,	FACTOREM	CAELI
I believe	in	one	God,	the Father	all-powerful,	maker	of heaven

ET	TERRAE,	VISIBILIUM	OMNIUM	ET	INVISIBILIUM.	ET	IN	UNUM
and	of earth,	visible	of all things	and	invisible.	And	in	one

DOMINUM	JESUM	CHRISTUM,	FILIUM	DEI	UNIGENITUM,	ET	EX	PATRE
Lord	Jesus	Christ	Son	of God	only-begotten,	and	from	the Father

NATUM	ANTE	OMNIA	SAECULA.	DEUM	DE	DEO,	LUMEN	DE	LUMINE,
born	before	all	ages.	God	from	God,	light	from	light

DEUM	VERUM	DE	DEO	VERO,	GENITUM,	NON	FACTUM,	CONSUBSTANTIALEM
God	true	from	God	true,	begotten,	not	made,	of one substance

PATRI:	PER	QUEM	OMNIA	FACTA	SUNT.	QUI	PROPTER	NOS	HOMINES
with the Father:	through	whom[1]	all things	made	were.	Who	on account of	us	men

ET	PROPTER	NOSTRAM	SALUTEM	DESCENDIT	DE	CAELIS.	ET	INCARNATUS
and	on account of	our	salvation	he came down	from	heaven.	And	incarnate

EST	DE	SPIRITU	SANCTO	EX	MARIA	VIRGINE:	ET	HOMO	FACTUS	EST.
was	of	the Spirit	Holy	from	Mary	Virgin:	and	man	made	was.

CRUCIFIXUS	ETIAM	PRO	NOBIS:	SUB	PONTIO	PILATO	PASSUS,
(He was) crucified	also	for	us:	under	Pontius	Pilate	suffered

ET	SEPULTUS	EST.	ET	RESURREXIT	TERTIA	DIE,	SECUNDUM	SCRIPTURAS.
and	buried	he was.	And	he rose again	third	on the day,	according to	the scriptures.

ET	ASCENDIT	IN	CAELUM:	SEDET	AD	DEXTERAM	PATRIS.
And	ascended	into	Heaven:	he sits	at	the right hand	of the Father

ET	ITERUM	VENTURUS	EST	CUM	GLORIA	JUDICARE	VIVOS	ET	MORTUOS:
and	again	about to come	he is	with	glory	to judge	the living	and	the dead:

CUJUS	REGNI	NON	ERIT	FINIS.	ET	IN	SPIRITUM	SANCTUM,	DOMINUM
of whose[2]	kingdom	not	there will be	an end.	And	in	the Spirit	Holy,	the Lord

ET	VIVIFICANTEM:	QUI	EX	PATRE	FILIOQUE	PROCEDIT.	QUI	CUM
and	life-giving:	who	from	the Father	and the Son	proceeds.	Who	with

PATRE	ET	FILIO	SIMUL	ADORATUR,	ET	CONGLORIFICATUR:	QUI
the Father	and	the Son	at the same time	is adored,	and	is glorified:	who

LOCUTUS	EST	PER	PROPHETAS.	ET	UNAM	SANCTAM	CATHOLICAM
spoke		through	the prophets.	And	one	holy	catholic

ET	APOSTOLICAM	ECCLESIAM.	CONFITEOR	UNUM	BAPTISMA	IN	REMISSIONEM
and	apostolic	Church.	I confess (acknowledge)	one	baptism	into (for)	the forgiveness

PECCATORUM.	ET	EXSPECTO	RESURRECTIONEM	MORTUORUM,	ET	VITAM
of sins.	And	I look forward to	the resurrection	of the dead,	and	the life

VENTURI	SAECULI.	AMEN.
about to come	of the world.	Amen.

[1] i.e. the Son   [2] i.e. his

SANCTUS,	SANCTUS,	SANCTUS	DOMINUS	DEUS	SABAOTH[3].	PLENI	SUNT
Holy,	holy,	holy	Lord	God	of great armies.	Full	are

CAELI	ET	TERRA	GLORIA	TUA.	HOSANNA[4]	IN	EXCELSIS.	BENEDICTUS
the heavens	and	the earth	with glory	your.	Hosanna	in	the highest.	Blessed

QUI	VENIT	IN	NOMINE	DOMINI.	HOSANNA	IN	EXCELSIS.
who	comes	in	the name	of the Lord.	Hosanna	in	the highest.

PATER	NOSTER,	QUI	ES	IN	CAELIS:	SANCTIFICETUR	NOMEN
Father	our,	who	are	in	heaven:	may (it) be hallowed	name

TUUM;	ADVENIAT	REGNUM	TUUM;	FIAT	VOLUNTAS	TUA,	SICUT
your;	may (it) come	kingdom	your;	may (it) be done	will	your,	as

IN	CAELO,	ET	IN	TERRA.	PANEM	NOSTRUM	QUOTIDIANUM
in	heaven,	and (so)	in (on)	earth.	Bread	our	of each day

DA	NOBIS	HODIE;	ET	DIMITTE	NOBIS	DEBITA	NOSTRA,	SICUT
give	to us	today;	and	forgive	(to) us	offences	our,	as

ET	NOS	DIMITTIMUS	DEBITORIBUS	NOSTRIS;	ET	NE	NOS
also	we	forgive	those who offend	(against) us;	and	(do) not	us

INDUCAS	IN	TENTATIONEM;	SED	LIBERA	NOS	A	MALO.
lead	into	temptation;	but	deliver	us	from	evil.

AGNUS	DEI,	QUI	TOLLIS	PECCATA	MUNDI:	MISERERE	NOBIS. (twice)
Lamb	of God,	who	take away	the sins	of the world:	have mercy	on us.

AGNUS	DEI,	QUI	TOLLIS	PECCATA	MUNDI:	DONA	NOBIS	PACEM.
Lamb	of God,	who	take away	the sins	of the world:	give	to us	peace.

[3] and [4]:Hebrew words.

Note: KYRIE ELEISON – a fragment of Greek

In the early days of the Church the liturgy was in Greek. By the end of the 4th century Latin had replaced Greek in the Western Church, and only a few fragments of the liturgy are in Greek. On Good Friday, during the Veneration of the Cross, the Reproaches are sung alternately in Greek and Latin, and at Rome on solemn occasions some readings are chanted in both Greek and Latin. But the most familiar piece of Greek is KYRIE ELEISON. The Latin equivalent would be 'Dómine, miserére'.

KYRIE,	ELEISON
Lord,	have mercy

CHRISTE,	ELEISON
Christ,	have mercy

KYRIE,	ELEISON
Lord,	have mercy

'Can you still say the Mass in Latin? The tide is turning ...'

Gavdeamus Omnes in Domino

PLAN OF SECTIONS

Section A

STATEMENT

Page

Section E

PROPER NOUNS

Answers

Vocabulary

*'Beginners on the left, old hands on the right, and the rest of you
say for your penance a Pater, an Ave and a Gloria.'*

Section A

1. LAUDÁMUS TE

We praise you

English pronouns: I, YOU, HE etc. are usually found in front of the verb — I love. In Latin these are added to the end of the verb root, usually with the help of a connecting vowel.

LAUD**O**	— I praise	LAUD**AMUS**	— WE praise
LAUD**AS**	— YOU* praise	LAUD**ATIS**	— YOU (p.) praise
LAUD**AT**	— HE/SHE praises	LAUD**ANT**	— THEY praise

* formerly 'thou', to distinguish it from the plural 'you'.

NOTE: the *infinitive* is made up of the ROOT, connecting letter + RE, so LAUD**ARE** — to praise.

VOCABULARY

ADÓRO, adoráre	— to adore	ROGO, rogáre	— to ask
GLORÍFICO, glorificáre	— to glorify	REGNO, regnáre	— to reign
EXSPÉCTO, exspectáre	— to await	SPERO, speráre	— to hope

Verbs using '*A*' as their connecting letter belong to the first conjugation (or family) of verbs.

The SECOND conjugation has 'E' as its connecting letter: PLAC*E*RE — to please

PLAC**E**O	— I please	PLAC**E**MUS	— WE please
PLAC**E**S	— YOU please	PLAC**E**TIS	— YOU please
PLAC**E**T	— HE/SHE pleases	PLAC**E**NT	— THEY please

NOTE: same *personal endings* as for LAUDO

VOCABULARY

VÍDEO, vidére	— to see	JÚBEO, jubére	— to command
SÉDEO, sedére	— to sit	RÉPLEO, replére	— to fill

Exercise 1.

Translate the verbs underlined in these phrases, and identify the conjugation to which they belong. (The answers and translation of the whole phrase are in the Answers.)

1. Laudámus te.

2. Adorámus te.

3. Qui tecum vivit et regnat per ómnia saécula saeculórum.

4. Qui sedes ad déxteram Patris.

5. Rex bone, cui bona cuncta placent.

6. Qui vivis et regnas cum Deo Patre.

7. In te sperámus, Dómine.

8. Glorificámus te.

9. Et exspécto resurrectiónem mortuórum.

10. Rogámus ac pétimus.

2. BENEDÍCIMUS TE
We bless you

The THIRD conjugation adds the usual personal endings to the connecting letter 'I' in all but the first and last persons.

REGO	— I rule	**REG*I*MUS**	— WE rule
REG*I*S	— YOU rule	**REG*I*TIS**	— YOU rule
REG*I*T	— HE/SHE rules	**REGUNT**	— THEY rule

VOCABULARY

BENEDÍCO, benedícere	— to bless	DUCO, dúcere	— to lead
VIVO, vívere	— to live	CONCÉDO, concédere	— to grant
RESÚRGO. resúrgere	— to rise again.		

The FOURTH conjugation also uses the connecting letter 'I' in ALL persons, adding 'U' in the last.

AUD*I*O	— I hear	**AUD*I*MUS**	— WE hear
AUD*I*S	— YOU hear	**AUD*I*TIS**	— YOU hear
AUD*I*T	— HE/SHE hears	**AUD*I*UNT**	— THEY hear

VOCABULARY

EXAÚDIO, exaudíre	— to hear graciously	VÉNIO, veníre	— to come
CUSTÓDIO, custodíre	— to guard, keep	SÉNTIO, sentíre	— to feel

The FIFTH conjugation (sometimes called the 'mixed conjugation') has exactly the same connecting letters as the fourth in the present tense, but 'E' in the infinitive.

ACCIP*I*O	— I take	**ACCIP*I*MUS**	— WE take
ACCIP*I*S	— YOU take	**ACCIP*I*TIS**	— YOU take
ACCIP*I*T	— HE/SHE takes	**ACCIP*I*UNT**	— THEY take

VOCABULARY

RECÍPIO, recípere	— to receive	RESPÍCIO, respícere	— to look at
FÁCIO, fácere	— to make or do	PROFÍCIO, proficere	— to avail, to further

Exercise 2.

Translate the verbs underlined in these phrases, and identify the conjugation to which they belong, as in Exercise 1.

1. <u>Benedícimus</u> te.

2. Qui tecum <u>vivit</u> et <u>regnat</u> per ómnia saécula saeculórum.

3. Christus <u>resúrgit</u> hódie.

4. Benedíctus qui <u>venit</u> in nómine Dómini.

5. Sine discretióne <u>sentímus</u>.

6. Fidélibus tuis dignánter <u>concédis</u>.

7. <u>Dico</u> ego ópera mea regi.

8. Fidem Ecclésiae tuae <u>réspicis</u>.

9. Dóminus Deus noster humília <u>réspicit</u>.

10. Corpus Christi <u>custódit</u> me in vitam aetérnam.

3. PRO ECCLÉSIA TUA SANCTA

For your holy Church

ECCLESIA: Church. 1st declension noun, feminine, singular.

The endings of Latin nouns change according to the job they are doing in a sentence. These functions are called *cases*.

Here is the word ECCLÉSIA in its six cases in the singular:

Nominative (subject)	ECCLESIA	— church
Vocative (address)	ECCLESIA	— O church
Accusative (direct object)	ECCLESIAM	— church
Genitive (possessive)	ECCLESIAE	— of the church
Dative ('to', 'for')	ECCLESIAE	— to or for the church
Ablative ('by', 'with', 'from')	ECCLESIA	— by, with or from the church

As families of verbs are called *conjugations* so families of nouns are called *declensions*. ECCLESIA belongs to the first of five declensions.

Natural gender distinguishes between male and female: prophéta (prophet, masculine), regína (queen, feminine).

Words denoting things, abstract or concrete, have a *grammatical gender* which is either masculine, feminine or neuter. Most nouns in the first declension are, like ecclésia, feminine.

NOTE: Papa, masculine: Pope.

VOCABULARY

TERRA, terrae (f)	— earth, land	ÁNIMA, ánimae (f)	— soul
CULPA, culpae (f)	— fault	AQUA, aquae (f)	— water
GRÁTIA, grátiae (f)	— grace	MISERICÓRDIA, misericórdiae (f)	— mercy

NOTE: The articles 'the' and 'a' do not exist in Latin.

Exercise 3.

Give the meaning, gender and possible cases of these words (The first one is done for you):

1. Ecclésia: Church, feminine, nom. voc. abl., sing.

2. misericórdia.

3. culpa.

4. aquam.

5. grátia.

6. vitam.

7. ánimam.

8. terrae.

9. ecclésiae.

10. vitae.

4. IN ECCLÉSIIS BENEDÍCAM TE, DÓMINE

In the churches I will bless you, Lord.

ECCLÉSIAE — churches, 1st declension noun, feminine plural

Nom.	ECCLESI**AE**	— churches (subject)
Voc.	ECCLESI**AE**	— O churches
Acc.	ECCLESI**AS**	— churches (object)
Gen.	ECCLESI**ARUM**	— of the churches
Dat.	ECCLESI**IS**	— to or for the churches
Abl.	ECCLESI**IS**	— by, with or from the churches

VOCABULARY

SCRIPTÚRA, scriptúrae (f)	— scripture	PORTA, portae (f)	— gate
LINGUA, linguae (f)	— tongue, language	GRÁTIAE, gratiárum (f.p)	— thanks
PROPHÉTA, prophétae (m*)	— prophet		

* gender follows sex where possible.

Exercise 4 (Answer as for Exercise 3).

1. portae.

2. terrárum.

3. prophétas.

4. linguis.

5. ecclésiis.

6. scriptúras.

7. ánimae.

8. grátias.

9. línguis.

10. animárum.

5. CANTÁBO DÓMINO

I will sing to the Lord

> STATEMENT

In the FUTURE TENSE the connecting letters are different: the personal endings are virtually the same as in the present tense.

1st conjugation: LAUDABO

LAUD*A*BO	— I shall praise	LAUD*A*BIMUS	— WE shall praise
LAUD*A*BIS	— YOU will praise	LAUD*A*BITIS	— YOU will praise
LAUD*A*BIT	— HE/SHE will praise	LAUD*A*BUNT	— THEY will praise

2nd conjugation (note different connecting letters, but same personal endings): PLACEBO

PLAC*E*BO	— I shall please	PLAC*E*BIMUS	— WE shall please
PLAC*E*BIS	— YOU will please	PLAC*E*BITIS	— YOU will please
PLACEBIT	— HE/SHE will please	PLACEBUNT	— THEY will please

Exercise 5. (From now on you will need to use the full vocabulary at the end of the book.)
Translate and name the conjugations of the underlined verbs; the meaning of the whole phrase will be given in the Answers.

1. Te sine fine <u>laudábimus</u>.

2. <u>Regnábit</u> super nos Salvátor mundi.

3. <u>Vidébit</u> omnis caro salutáre Dei nostri.

4. <u>Adorábo</u> ad templum sanctum tuum.

5. <u>Invocábo</u> nomen Dómini.

6. Beáti mundo corde, quóniam ipsi Deum <u>vidébunt</u>.

7. Beáti mites, quóniam ipsi <u>possidébunt</u> terram.

8. <u>Revelábit</u> Dóminus condénsa.

9. <u>Cantábo</u> Dómino, qui bona tríbuit mihi.

10. In die mala <u>liberábit</u> paúperem Dóminus.

6. BENEDÍCAM DÓMINO

I shall bless the Lord.

STATEMENT

3rd conjugation: REGAM* (careful!) A different pattern in the connecting letter — but familiar personal endings except note alternative ending * for 'I'.

REG*A*M*	— I shall rule	REG*E*MUS	—WE shall rule
REG*E*S	— YOU will rule	REG*E*TIS	—YOU will rule
REG*E*T	— HE/SHE will rule	REG*E*NT	—THEY will rule

4th conjugation: *AUDIAM*. Connecting letters are similar to the third conjugation but with an 'i' in front.

AUD*I*AM	— I shall hear	AUD*I*EMUS	— WE shall hear
AUD*I*ES	— YOU will hear	AUD*I*ETIS	— YOU will hear
AUD*I*ET	— HE/SHE will hear	AUD*I*ENT	— THEY will hear

5th (or 'mixed') conjugation: *ACCIPIAM*.

ACCIP*I*AM	— I shall take	ACCIP*I*EMUS	— WE shall take
ACCIP*I*ES	— YOU will take	ACCIP*I*ETIS	— YOU will take
ACCIP*I*ET	— HE/SHE will take	ACCIP*I*ENT	— THEY will take

Exercise 6.

Translate and name the conjugations of the underlined verbs; the meaning of the whole phrase will be given in the Answers.

1. Omnis terra psalmum <u>dicet</u> nómini tuo, Altíssime.

2. In templo eius omnes <u>dicent</u> glóriam.

3. <u>Vivam</u>, et <u>narrábo</u> ópera Dómini.

4. Vultum tuum, Dómine, <u>requíram</u>.

5. Non vos <u>relínquam</u> órphanos: <u>véniam</u> ad vos íterum, allelúia.

6. Hic Jesus, qui assúmptus est a vobis in caelum, sic <u>véniet</u>.

7. Daemónia <u>ejícient</u>: super agros manus <u>impónent</u> et bene <u>habébunt</u>.

8. In die resurrectiónis meae, <u>praecédam</u> vos in Galilaéam.

9. Quis <u>ascéndet</u> in montem Dómini, aut quis <u>stabit</u> in loco sancto eius?

10. Hic <u>accípiet</u> benedictiónem a Dómino.

7. ÁNGELUS DÓMINI ANNUNTIÁVIT MARÍAE

The Angel of the Lord declared unto Mary.

ÁNGELUS — Angel. Second declension noun, masculine, singular.

Nom.	ANGEL**US**	— angel (subject)
Voc.	ANGEL**E**	— O angel
Acc.	ANGEL**UM**	— angel (object)
Gen.	ANGEL**I**	— OF an angel
Dat.	ANGEL**O**	— TO, FOR an angel
AbI.	ANGEL**O**	— BY, WITH or FROM an angel

VOCABULARY

AGNUS, agni (m)	— lamb (voc. agnus)	DEUS, Dei (m)	— God (voc. Deus)
FÍLIUS, fílii (m)	— son (voc. fili)	DÓMINUS, Dómini (m)	— Lord
SERVUS, servi (m)	— servant		

NOTE: The genitive singular is always given in the vocabulary to show the *declension* to which the word belongs. Compare ECCLESI**A**, ECCLESI**AE** — first declension.

Exercise 7.

Give the gender and case of the underlined nouns; translate if you can!

1. <u>Agnus Dei</u>, qui tollis peccáta mundi, miserére nobis.

2. Grátias agámus <u>Dómino Deo</u> nostro.

3. Oráre pro me ad <u>Dóminum Deum</u> nostrum.

4. <u>Deum</u> verum de <u>Deo</u> vero.

5. Nunc dimíttis <u>servum</u> tuum, <u>Dómine</u>.

6. <u>Dóminus</u> in <u>loco</u> sancto eius.*

7. Per <u>Dóminum</u> nostrum Jesum <u>Christum Fílium</u> tuum.

8. Per manus sancti <u>Ángeli</u> tui…

9. <u>Ángelus Dómini</u> annuntiávit Maríae.

10. <u>Dómine Deus,</u> rex caeléstis.

* 'is' is often left out in Latin.

8. CUM ÁNGELIS ET ARCHÁNGELIS

With Angels and Archangels.

ÁNGELI — Angels. Second declension noun, masculine, plural.

Nom.	ANGEL**I**	— angels (subject)
Voc.	ANGEL**I**	— O angels
Acc.	ANGEL**OS**	— angels (object)
Gen.	ANGEL**ORUM**	— OF angels
Dat.	ANGEL**IS**	— TO, FOR angels
Abl.	ANGEL**IS**	— BY, WITH or FROM angels.

VOCABULARY

APÓSTOLUS, apóstoli (m)	— apostle
ARCHÁNGELUS, archángeli (m)	— archangel
CAELI, caelórum (m. plural)	— heaven

DISCÍPULUS, discípuli (m)   — disciple
FÁMULUS, fámuli (m)   — servant
HYMNUS, hymni (m)   — hymn
ÍNFERI, inferórum (m. plural)   — the lower regions, the dead, hell

Exercise 8.

Answer as for Exercise 7.

1. Beáti <u>apóstoli</u> Petrus et Paulus.

2. Nobis quoque peccatóribus <u>fámulis</u> tuis, donáre dignéris.

3. Pleni sunt <u>caeli</u> et <u>terra glória</u> tua.

4. Lauda Sion Salvatórem . . . in <u>hymnis</u> et cánticis.

5. <u>Christi</u> descénsum ad <u>ínferos</u> recólimus.

6. <u>Dómine</u>, ad te levávi <u>óculos</u> meos.

7. Unde et mémores nos <u>servi</u> tui, <u>Dómine</u> .

8. Benedixit, deditque <u>discípulis</u> suis.

9. Cum tuis sanctis <u>Apóstolis</u> et martýribus.

10. Majestátem tuam laudant <u>Ángeli</u>, adórant Dominatiónes, <u>caeli caelorúmque</u>* concélebrant.

*que on the end of a word means 'and': e.g. Filio<u>que</u> - and from the Son.

9. PUER NATUS EST NOBIS

Unto us a boy is born

PUER — Boy   VIR — Man   Second declension nouns, masculine, singular and plural.

Both these omit 'US + 'E' in the nominative and vocative singular, but are otherwise regular.

Nom.	PUER	— boy (subject)	PUERI	— boys (subject)
Voc.	PUER	— O boy	PUERI	— O boys
Acc.	PUER**UM**	— boy (object)	PUER**OS**	— boys (object)
Gen.	PUER**I**	— OF the boy	PUER**ORUM**	— OF the boys
Dat.	PUER**O**	— TO, or FOR the boy	PUER**IS**	— TO or FOR the boys
Abl.	PUER**O**	— BY, WITH or FROM the boy	PUER**IS**	— BY, WITH or FROM the boys

NOTE: Some -ER second declension nouns drop the 'E': e.g. mágister, mágistri (m).

Exercise 9.

Try to translate all of the following sentences. These are adapted from material in the Missal (remember to use the main vocabulary).

1. Viri Deum timent.

2. Discípuli Dómini hymnum cantábunt.

3. Dóminus púerum amat.

4. Ángeli Dóminum adórant.

5. Óculi apostolorum Dóminum respíciunt.

6. Archángeli Fílium Dei laudant.

7. Discípuli ínferos timent.

8. Prophétae misericórdiam exspéctant.

9. Fámuli Dómini hymnum aúdient.

10. Deus ecclésiam grátia munit.

10. ET VERBUM CARO FACTUM EST

And the Word was made flesh..

VERBUM — word. Second declension noun, neuter, singular and plural.

Nom.	VERB**UM**	— word (subject)	VERB**A**
Voc.	VERB**UM**	— O word etc.	VERB**A**
Acc.	VERB**UM**		VERB**A**
Gen.	VERB**I**		VERB**ORUM**
Dat.	VERB**O**		VERB**IS**
AbI.	VERB**O**		VERB**IS**

VOCABULARY

AUXÍLIUM, auxílii (n)	— help
DONUM, doni (n)	— gift
EVANGÉLIUM, evangélii (n)	— gospel
PECCÁTUM, peccáti (n)	— sin
SACRAMÉNTUM, sacraménti (n)	— sacrament
REGNUM, regni (n)	— kingdom
SACRIFÍCIUM, sacrifícii (n)	— sacrifice
SAÉCULUM, saéculi (n)	— world, age
VINUM, vini (n)	— wine

Exercise 10.

Try to translate the whole sentence, as before.

1. Servi Dómini dona portant.

2. Sacrifícium Dóminus súscipit.

3. In saécula saeculórum.

4. Apóstolus evangélium núntiat.

5. Verbum Dómini: Deo grátias.

6. Advéniat (may it come) regnum tuum.

7. Dicit María: Vinum non habent.

8. Auxílium meum (my) a Dómino ('is' understood).

9. Agnus Dei, qui tollis (who take away) peccáta mundi.

10. Adorémus (let us adore) in aetérnum sanctíssimum sacraméntum (most holy).

11. SEMPER ET UBÍQUE GRÁTIAS ÁGERE

…always and everywhere to give thanks …

ADVERBS describe and modify verbs, and also adjectives and other adverbs. They answer the questions: how, when, where, how much?

VOCABULARY

'How?'

DIGNE	— worthily	CONFIDÉNTER	— confidently
MIRABÍLITER	— wonderfully	FELICITER	— happily
BENE	— well		

'When?'

ADHUC	— still	NUNC	— now
SEMPER	— always	HÓDIE	— today
ÍTERUM	— again	PRÍDIE	— the day before
SIMUL	— at the same time		

'Where?'

UBIQUE	— everywhere	SURSUM	— upwards
HIC	— here	SUPRA	— over, above

'How much?' ('To what extent?')

TAM	— so	NIMIS	— very much, too much
TANTUM	— only	QUOTQUOT	— as many as

Exercise 11. Translate:

1. Dóminus servum semper amat.

2. Ángeli Deum hódie adórant.

3. Rex confidénter orábat.

4. Ecclésia evangélium hic et ubíque proclámat.

5. Nunc dimíttis servum tuum (your), Dómine.

6. Verbum Dei felíciter accípimus.

7. Dóminus Ecclésiam fidéliter custódit.

8. Dómine, peccávi (I have sinned) nimis.

9. Dómine, tantum dic (say) verbo et sanábitur (will be healed) ánima mea.

10. Dóminus mirabíliter resurgébat: nunc vere vivit.

NOTE the following from the Ordinary of the Mass:

Confiteor Deo ... quia peccávi *nimis.*
I confess to God ... that I have sinned *very much.*

Et *íterum* ventúrus est cum glória.
And he will come *again* with glory.

Cum Patre et Fílio *simul* adorátur.
With the Father and the Son he is *at the same time* (simultaneously) adored.

Sursum corda.
('Lift' understood) upwards (your) hearts.

'Personally I prefer the Missa de Angelis*'*

12. CLAMÁBAT: LÁZARE, VENI FORAS

He cried out: "Lazarus, come forth"

 *STATEMENT*

The IMPERFECT tense expresses continued, repetitive or habitual actions. It is rarely found in the Missal, but be able to recognise it.

1st. conj: LAUD*ABA*M etc.
2nd. conj: PLAC*EBA*M etc.
3rd. conj: REG*EBA*M etc.
4th. conj: AUDI*EBA*M etc.
5th. conj: ACCIPI*EBA*M etc.

Exercise 12.

Translate the underlined verb: the rest of the sentence will be given in the Answers.

1. Púeri in mánibus portábant ramos.

2. Clamábant voce magna, dicéntes: Hosánna in excélsis.

3. Púeri Hebraeórum vestiménta prosternébant in via, dicéntes: Hosánna fílio David.

4. Dixit Jesus: Ego servábam eos, quos dedísti mihi.

5. Multitúdo languéntium veniébat ad eum; et sanábat omnes.

6. Providébam Deum in conspéctu meo semper.

7. Oportébat (impersonal verb: it was necessary) Christum pati, et resúrgere a mórtuis tértia die.

8. Cum esses júnior (a young man), cingébas te, et ambulábas ubi volébas.

9. Senex púerum portábat; puer autem senem regébat.

10. Ignis ille super discipulos apparébat.

13. SANCTUS, SANCTUS, SANCTUS

Holy, holy, holy …

ADJECTIVES Type 1
All ADJECTIVES have the *same* number, gender and case as the nouns they describe.

There is a large number of adjectives where the *masculine* endings are like *dóminus*, the *feminine* endings are like *ecclésia*, and the *neuter* endings are like *verbum*.

Sanctus, a, um — holy

Singular

	M.	F.	N.
Nom.	SANCTUS	SANCTA	SANCTUM
Voc.	SANCTE	SANCTA	SANCTUM
Acc.	SANCTUM	SANCTAM	SANCTUM
Gen.	SANCTI	SANCTAE	SANCTI
Dat.	SANCTO	SANCTAE	SANCTO
AbI.	SANCTO	SANCTA	SANCTO

Plural

	M.	F.	N.
Nom.	SANCTI	SANCTAE	SANCTA
Voc.	SANCTI	SANCTAE	SANCTA
Acc.	SANCTOS	SANCTAS	SANCTA

Gen.	SANCT**ORUM**	SANCT**ARUM**	SANCT**ORUM**
Dat.	SANCT**IS**	SANCT**IS**	SANCT**IS**
Abl.	SANCT**IS**	SANCT**IS**	SANCT**IS**

Sanctus Dóminus — Holy Lord   Sancta Ecclésia — Holy Church
Sanctum verbum   Holy word

VOCABULARY

SOLUS, a, um	— alone, only	APOSTÓLICUS, a, um	— apostolic
UNUS, a, um	— one	BENEDÍCTUS, a, um	— blessed
VERUS, a, um	— true	DIGNUS, a, um	— worthy, fitting
JUSTUS, a, um	— right	NOSTER, nostra, nostrum	— our
UNIGÉNITUS, a, um	— only begotten	CATHÓLICUS, a, um	— catholic

Exercise 13. Translate:

1. Tu solus sanctus.

2. Sanctum evangélium tuum nuntiábo.

3. Credo in unum Dóminum Jesum Christum.

4. Fílium Dei unigénitum.

5. Deum verum de Deo vero.

6. Et in Spíritum Sanctum.

7. Et in unam, sanctam, cathólicam et apostólicam Ecclésiam.

8. Benedíctus Deus in saécula.

9. Dignum et justum est grátias ágere (to give thanks) Dómino Deo nostro (our).

10. Dómine, non sum (I am) dignus.

14. EGO SUM PANIS VITAE

I am the bread of life

STATEMENT

ESSE: To be

PRESENT TENSE — note the familiar personal endings.

SUM	— I am	**SUMUS**	— WE are
ES	— YOU are	**ESTIS**	— YOU are
EST	— HE is	**SUNT**	— THEY are

1. ESSE is not followed by the accusative case but by a nominative *complement*: Ego sum via, véritas, vita — I am the way, the truth and the life.
2. Very often the verb 'to be' is taken for granted and therefore left out: Benedíctus Deus in saécula — Blessed (be) God for ever.

VOCABULARY

ET	— and	IN + abl. case	— in
TUUS, a, um	— your	ADSUM	— I am present

Exercise 14. Translate:

1. Dómine, non sum dignus.

2. Benedíctus es, Dómine, Deus univérsi.

3. Hoc est corpus meum ... hic est calix ...

4. Pleni sunt caeli et terra glória tua.

5. Benedíctus Deus et Pater Dómini nostri Jesu Christi. (see note 2, above)

6. Tu solus sanctus, tu solus Dóminus. (see note 2)

7. Mystérium fídei.

8. Vere sanctus es, Dómine.

9. Pater noster, qui es in caelis.

10. Cum voto et hymnis, ádsumus coram te.

15. QUI ERAT ET ERIT

Who was and who will be

STATEMENT

IMPERFECT TENSE of verb To be — note endings like LAUDABAM (see Lesson 12).

ER**AM**	— I was	ER**AMUS**	— WE were
ER**AS**	— YOU were	ER**ATIS**	— YOU were
ER**AT**	— HE was	ER**ANT**	— THEY were

FUTURE TENSE — note endings like LAUDABO (see Lesson 5).

ER**O**	— I shall be	ER**IMUS**	— WE shall be
ER**IS**	— YOU will be	ER**ITIS**	— YOU will be
ER**IT**	— HE will be	ER**UNT**	— THEY will be

Exercise 15. Translate:

1. In mundo erat, et mundus eum (him) non cognóvit (recognise).
2. Servi non éritis, sed amíci.
3. Apóstoli discípuli Dómini erant.
4. Servi Dómini erámus.
5. Christus Dóminus semper erit.
6. Sancti semper beáti erunt.
7. Deus, justus et magnus semper eris.
8. Scriptúrae sanctae in ecclésiis erant.
9. Amíci Christi sumus.
10. Christus Dóminus erat, est, erit.

16. UNA CUM PAPA NOSTRO

Together with our Pope

ADJECTIVES: AGREEMENT

Nouns and adjectives often have the same endings (un*am*, sanct*am*, catholic*am* et apostolic*am*) when the declension and gender follow the usual patterns. But a noun such as PAPA, papae (Pope) although first declension, is *masculine* in gender, so its adjective declines like *sanctus*.

PAPA SANCTUS — Holy Pope

	S		P	
Nom.	**PAPA**	**SANCTUS**	**PAPAE**	**SANCTI**
Voc.	**PAPA**	**SANCTE**	**PAPAE**	**SANCTI**
Acc.	**PAPAM**	**SANCTUM**	**PAPAS**	**SANCTOS**
Gen.	**PAPAE**	**SANCTI**	**PAPARUM**	**SANCTORUM**
Dat.	**PAPAE**	**SANCTO**	**PAPIS**	**SANCTIS**
Abl.	**PAPA**	**SANCTO**	**PAPIS**	**SANCTIS**

VOCABULARY

PAPA, papae (m)	— Pope	PROPHÉTA, prophétae (m)	— prophet
BAPTISTA, Baptístae (m)	— Baptist	PATRIÁRCHA, patriárchae (m)	— patriarch

Exercise 16. Translate:

1. Offérimus haec dona pro Ecclésia tua sancta una (together) cum papa nostro N. (= nomen = name).

2. Acceptábas sacrifícium patriárchae nostri Abrahae (of Abraham).

3. Haec múnera in festivitáte (on the feast) beáti Joánnis (of John) Baptístae accéptas, Dómine.

4. Qui loctútus est (= who spoke) per prophétas sanctos.

5. Dómine, in prophéta beáto Joánne Baptísta tuam glóriam collaudámus.

17. ET HOMO FACTUS EST

And he was made man

THIRD DECLENSION NOUNS Type 1

These nouns can be *masculine*, *feminine* or *neuter* in gender.

There are several different nominative endings. Often the shape of the word changes when it declines.
The *genitive singular* shows the shape of the word: the case endings are added to the basic stem.
Look at HOMO, hóminis (masculine) — man.

HOMO nom. and voc. sing.	HOMIN is STEM for rest of declension	IS gen. sing. ending

		Singular		*Plural*	
Nom.	HOMO	— man (subject)	HOMINES	— men (subject)
Voc.	HOMO	— O man	HOMINES	— O men
Acc.	HOMINEM	— man (object)	HOMINES	— men (object)
Gen.	HOMINIS	— OF man	HOMINUM	— OF men
Dat.	HOMINI	— TO or FOR man	HOMINIBUS	— TO, FOR men
Abl.	HOMINE	— BY, WITH or FROM man	HOMINIBUS	— BY, WITH or FROM men

Now look at a neuter noun: NOMEN, nóminis (neuter) — name. Look back to VERBUM (section 10). Note that (1) ALL NEUTER nouns remain the *same* in the Nom. and Acc.; (2) that they all end in 'A' in the plural.

		Singular		*Plural*	
Nom.	NOMEN	— a name (subject)	NOMINA	— names (subject)
Voc.	NOMEN	— O name	NOMINA	— O names
Acc.	NOMEN	— a name (object)	NOMINA	— names (object)
Gen.	NOMINIS	— OF a name	NOMINUM	— OF names
Dat.	NOMINI	— TO or FOR a name	NOMINIBUS	— TO or FOR names
Abl.	NOMINE	— BY, WITH or FROM a name	NOMINIBUS	— BY, WITH or FROM names

VOCABULARY

CALIX, cálicis (m)	— chalice, cup	CORPUS, córporis (n)	— body
SANGUIS, sánguinis (m)	— blood	LUMEN, lúminis (n)	— light
PATER, patris (m)	— father	FRATER, fratris (m)	— brother
FACTOR, factóris (m)	— maker	MORS, mortis (f)	— death
OPUS, óperis (n)	— work	BAPTISMA, baptismatis (n)	— baptism
NOTE: many abstract nouns:		COGITÁTIO, cogitatiónis (f)	— thought
OMÍSSIO, omissiónis (f)	— omission	REMÍSSIO, remissiónis (f)	— remission
RESURRÉCTIO, resurrectiónis (f)	— resurrection	VOLÚNTAS, voluntátis (f)	— will

Exercise 17.

Translate:

1. Hic est calix sánguinis mei.

2. Hoc est corpus meum.

3. In nómine Patris et Fílii et Spíritus Sancti. Amen.

4. Peccávi nimis cogitatióne, verbo, ópere et omissióne.

5. Ideo precor (I beseech) beátam Maríam semper Vírginem … et vos fratres, oráre (to pray) pro me …

6. Glória in excélsis Deo, et in terra pax homínibus bonae voluntátis.

7. Credo in unum Deum, Patrem omnipoténtem, factórem caeli et terrae …

8. Deum de Deo, lumen de lúmine.

9. Confíteor unum baptísma in remissiónem peccatórum.

10. Mortem tuam annuntiámus, Dómine, et tuam resurrectiónem confitémur …

Exercise 17a.

Underline all the *3rd declension nouns* in the 'Our Father'.

Pater noster, qui es in caelis, sanctificétur nomen tuum; advéniat regnum tuum; fiat volúntas tua, sicut in caelo et in terra. Panem nostrum quotidiánum da nobis hódie, et dimítte nobis débita nostra, sicut et nos dimíttimus debitóribus nostris. Et ne nos indúcas in tentatiónem, sed líbera nos a malo.

18. SINE FINE DICÉNTES, 'SANCTUS'

Without end saying 'Holy'

THIRD DECLENSION NOUNS *Type 2*

A. Some nouns in this declension insert 'i' in their genitive plural; many of them have the same number of syllables in the genitive singular as in the nominative.

FINIS, finis (m) — end

S.		P.	
Nom.	FINIS		FINES
Voc.	FINIS		FINES
Acc.	FINEM		FINES
Gen.	FINIS		FINIUM
Dat.	FINI		FINIBUS
Abl.	FINE		FINIBUS

B. Some neuter nouns in this declension have 'i' ablative singular endings; 'ia' nom and acc. plural endings.

ALTÁRE, altáris (n) — altar

VOCABULARY

IGNIS, ignis (m)	— fire	COR, cordis (n)	— heart
ORBIS, orbis (m)	— globe	MONS, montis (m)	— mountain
CARO, carnis (f)	— flesh	GENS, gentis (f)	— race, people
MENS, mentis (f)	— mind	NOX, noctis (f)	— night
NIX, nivis (f)	— snow		

Exercise 18.

Translate:

1. Qui (those who) confídunt in Dómino sunt sicut (like) mons Sion.

2. Veni, Sancte Spíritus, et tui amóris ignem in eis accénde (kindle).

3. Veni, lumen córdium.

4. Emítte lucem tuam et veritátem tuam: quae me addúcunt in montem sanctum tuum.

5. Spíritus Dómini replévit (has filled) orbem terrárum.

6. Illúmina (enlighten) corda nostra grátiae tuae splendóre.

7. Lavábis me… et super nivem dealbábor (I shall be made white).

8. Communicántes et noctem sacratíssimam (most holy) celebrántes.

9. Christus in veritáte carnis nostrae visibíliter (visibly) appáruit (appeared).

10. Veni, Sancte Spíritus... mentes tuórum vísita.

19. AD DÉXTERAM PATRIS

At the right hand of the Father

PREPOSITIONS 1

Many English *prepositions* are expressed in Latin by ENDINGS e.g. OF the Lord — DOMINI; AT night — NOCTE. But Latin also has PREPOSITIONS. They never change their endings. The nouns that follow them are in the *accusative* or *ablative* case.

PREPOSITIONS followed by the *accusative* case:

AD	— towards, to, at	ANTE	— before
APUD	— in the presence of	IN	— into
INTER	— among	PER	— through
POST	— after	PROPTER	— for the sake of
SECÚNDUM	— according to	SUPER	— upon, above

Exercise 19. Translate:

1. Accépit panem in sanctas ac venerábiles manus suas.

2. Qui propter nos hómines et propter nostram salútem descéndit de caelis.

3. Et resurréxit tértia die, secúndum scriptúras.

4. Et ascéndit in caelum, sedet ad déxteram Patris.

5. Oráte fratres ut meum ac vestrum sacrifícium acceptábile fiat (that it may become) apud Deum.

6. Qui sedes, Dómine, super Chérubim, éxcita poténtiam tuam, et veni.

7. Per Dóminum nostrum Jesum Christum. Amen.

8. Et ex Patre natum ante ómnia saécula.

9. Per crucem et resurrectiónem tuam liberásti (you have freed) nos.

10. Ad te Dómine levávi ánimam meam.

20. ... CUM IPSO, ET IN IPSO

with him, and in him

PREPOSITIONS 2

Prepositions followed by the *ablative* case.

EX	— from, away from, out of	CUM	— with
IN	— in, at, on	DE	— from, out of
SINE	— without	PRO	— for, on behalf of
CORAM	— in the presence of	A (AB before a word beginning with a vowel)	— by, from

Exercise 20. Translate:

1. Glória in excélsis Deo, et in terra pax homínibus.

2. Et ex Patre natum ante ómnia saécula.

3. Deum de Deo, lumen de lúmine, Deum verum de Deo vero.

4. Crucifíxus étiam pro nobis.

5. Qui cum Patre et Fílio simul adorátur (is adored) et conglorificátur (and is glorified).

6. Grátias ágimus quia (because) nos dignos habuísti (you have considered) astáre coram te.

7. Hymnum glóriae tuae cánimus, sine fine dicéntes, Sanctus...

8. Per ipsum, et cum ipso, et in ipso, est tibi Patri.. .omnis honor et glória.

9. A solis ortu (the rising) usque ad occásum oblátio munda offerátur nómini tuo.

10. Ipse enim in qua (that which) nocte tradebátur (he was betrayed) accépit panem.

21. QUIA PECCAVI NIMIS

Because I have sinned greatly

STATEMENT

PERFECT TENSE: *First and Second conjugations*

LAUDÁVI — I have praised
          I praised

Look at these *new* personal endings:

—	**I**	—	**IMUS**
—	**ISTI**	—	**ISTIS**
—	**IT**	—	**ERUNT**

These are added to the PERFECT STEM.
1st conjugation: Note characteristic 'AV' in stem:

LAUD*AVI*	— I have praised	LAUD*AV*IMUS	— WE have praised
LAUD*AV*ISTI	— YOU have praised	LAUD*AV*ISTIS	— YOU have praised
LAUD*AV*IT	— HE has praised	LAUD*AV*ERUNT	— THEY have praised

2nd conjugation: Note characteristic 'U' in the stem:

PLAC*U*I	— I have pleased	PLAC*U*IMUS	— WE have pleased
PLAC*U*ISTI	— YOU have pleased	PLAC*U*ISTIS	— YOU have pleased
PLAC*U*IT	— HE has pleased	PLAC*U*ERUNT	— THEY have pleased

NOTE three important *alternatives:*

1. LAUDAVISTI etc. sometimes shortened to LAUD**ASTI**
2. LAUDAVERUNT etc. sometimes shortened to LAUDA**VERE**
3. 'V' often omitted in 3rd plural — AUDIVER**UN**T becomes AUDIER**UN**T etc.

VOCABULARY

RÉNOVO, renovávi	— to renew	APPÁREO, appárui	— to appear
VIVÍFICO, vivificávi	— to give life to	RÉPLEO, replévi	— to fill
LEVO, levávi	— to raise, lift	MÉREO, mérui	— to deserve, merit
PARO, parávi	— to prepare	FUNDO, fundávi	— to found
ÍMPLEO, implévi	— to fulfil	EVANGELÍZO, evangelizávi	— to bring the good news to

Exercise 21. Translate:

1. Resúrgens (rising again) a morte (Christus) vitam renovávit.

2. In veritáte carnis nostrae (our) visibíliter appáruit.

3. Per mortem tuam (your) mundum vivificásti.

4. Spíritus Sanctus beátae Maríae víscera sua (his) virtúte replévit.

5. Ad te levávi ánimam meam (my), Dómine.

6. Per Vírginem Mariam merúimus Fílium tuum (your) auctórem vitae suscípere.

7. Réspice (look), Dómine, in hóstiam quam (which) Ecclésiae tuae ipse (you yourself) parásti.

8. Christus primo advéntu (coming) in humilitáte carnis, dispositiónis (order) antíquae munus implévit.

9. Christus salútem evangelizávit paupéribus, redemptiónem captívis, maestis corde laetítiam.

10. Tui sunt caeli, et tua est terra: orbem terrárum tu fundásti.

22. ACCÉPIT PANEM, BENEDÍXIT

He took bread, blessed it

STATEMENT

PERFECT TENSE: *Third, Fourth and Fifth Conjugations*

3rd conjugation: the largest group, with many different perfect stems

REXI	— I ruled	**REXIMUS**	— WE ruled
REXISTI	— YOU ruled	**REXISTIS**	— YOU ruled
REXIT	— HE ruled	**REXERUNT**	— THEY ruled

4th conjugation: note characteristic 'V' in stem

AUDIVI	— I heard	**AUDIVIMUS**	— WE heard
AUDIVISTI	— YOU heard	**AUDIVISTIS**	— YOU heard
AUDIVIT	— HE heard	**AUDIVERUNT**	— THEY heard

5th (or 'mixed') conjugation: all fifth conjugation perfect STEMS are *irregular:*

ACCEPI	— I took	**ACCEPIMUS**	— WE took
ACCEPISTI	— YOU took	**ACCEPISTIS**	— YOU took
ACCEPIT	— HE took	**ACCEPERUNT**	— THEY took

Exercise 22.

(n) Here is the opening paragraph of the fourth Eucharistic Prayer. It calls to mind all the great things that God has done for his people (and most of the verbs are third conjugation irregulars!). First underline all the verbs which have endings as above, then see if you can translate them. Use the vocabulary at the end of the book for both exercises.

Confitémur (we confess) tibi, Pater Sancte, quia (that) magnus es et ómnia ópera tua in sapiéntia et caritáte fecísti. Hóminem ad tuam imáginem condidísti, eique (and to him) commisísti mundi curam univérsi... Non eum dereliquísti in mortis império. Ómnibus enim misericórditer subvenísti... Sed et foédera plúries homínibus obtulisti (see OFFERO) eósque per prophétas erudísti in exspectatióne salútis ...

(b) Translate:

1. Vidi aquam egrediéntem de templo… et omnes ad quos (to whom) pervénit aqua ista salvi (saved) facti sunt.

2. Benedíctus es, Deus, quia de tua largitáte accépimus panem.

3. Meménto étiam fratrum nostrórum, qui in spe resurrectiónis dormiérunt.

4. Beáta María unigénitum tuum Sancti Spiritus obumbratióne concépit.

5. Benedíctus qui venísti in multitúdine misericórdiae tuae.

6. Accépit panem in sanctas ac venerábiles manus suas.

7. Subjécit pópulos nobis, et gentes sub pédibus nostris.

8. Et exsultávit spíritus meus in Deo salutári meo, quia respéxit humilitátem ancíllae suae.

9. Plebs Hebraéa tibi cum palmis óbviam venit.

10. Lutum fecit ex sputo Dóminus, et linívit óculos meos, et ábii (see ÁBEO) et lavi, et crédidi Deo.

NOTE: Do not worry too much about the conjugation to which these verbs belong.

The two *essential* things are to recognise:

1. The perfect endings,

2. The meaning of the verb which has changed its shape somewhat in the perfect tense.

23. VENTURUS EST CUM GLÓRIA JUDICARE

He is to come in glory to judge

STATEMENT

The INFINITIVE contains the *meaning* of the verb but no person is doing the action.

PRESENT		PAST	
LAUDÁRE	— to praise	LAUDAVÍSSE	— to have praised
PLACÉRE	— to please	PLACUÍSSE	— to have pleased
RÉGERE	— to rule	REXÍSSE	— to have ruled
AUDÍRE	— to hear	AUDIVÍSSE	— to have heard
ACCÍPERE	— to take	ACCEPÍSSE	— to have taken

Passive Present

LAUDÁRI	— to be praised
PLACÉRI	— to be pleased
REGI	— to be ruled
AUDÍRI	— to be heard
ACCÍPI	— to be taken

Uses:

1. The Infinitive completes the meaning of many verbs:
    Audémus *dicere* : Pater noster
    We dare *to say* : Our Father

2. Many adjectives are followed by the infinitive:
    Dignum et justum est grátias *ágere* …
    It is fitting and right *to give* thanks …

3. It is used to express purpose:

   Ventúrus est cum glória, *judícare* vivos et mórtuos.
   He is going to come again in glory, *to judge* the living and the dead.

4. It is used for indirect command:

   Ideo precor… vos, fratres, *oráre* pro me.
   And so I beseech you, brothers, *to pray* for me.

5. The Infinitive helps to confirm which *conjugation* the verb belongs to:

   LAUDO, LAUDÁRE : the 'A' confirms that the verb belongs to the 1st conjugation rather than the 3rd.
   PLÁCEO, PLACÉRE : the 'E' is characteristic of the 2nd conjugation.
   REGO, RÉGERE : absence of 'E' before the 'O' of rego distinguishes *rego, régere* from *pláceo, placére*; note also the accents.
   AÚDIO, AUDÍRE : characteristic 'I' of 4th conjugation.
   ACCÍPIO, ACCÍPERE : 'I' in present tense, 'E' in infinitive indicates the 5th conjugation.

Some verbs which are followed by an infinitive:

VÁLEO, valére	— to be able	JÚBEO, jubére	— to command
PERMÍTTO, permíttere	— to allow	DÉBEO, debére	— to have to, to be obliged
DÉSINO, desínere	— to cease	AÚDEO, audére	— to dare

Some adjectives are followed by an infinitive:

DIGNUS, digna, dignum	— fitting
JUSTUS, justa, justum	— right

Exercise 23.

Translate:

1. Christus missus est (was sent) sanáre contritos corde.

2. Vere dignum et justum est, aequum et salutáre, nos tibi semper et ubíque grátias ágere.

3. Munda (cleanse) cor meum ac lábia mea, ut (so that) sanctum evangélium tuum digne váleam (I may be able) nuntiáre.

4. Ecclésiam tuam pacificáre, custodíre, adunáre et régere dignéris (deign, grant) toto orbe terrárum.

5. Ab aetérna damnatióne nos éripi, et in electórum tuórum júbeas (command) grege numerári.

6. Vídimus stellam eius in oriénte, et vénimus cum munéribus adoráre Dóminum.

7. Fac (make) me tuis semper inhaerére mandátis, et a te nunquam separári permíttas (allow).

8. Hanc (this) igitur oblatiónem tibi offérimus pro his, quos (whom) regeneráre dignátus es (you have deigned) ex aqua et Spíritu Sancto.

9. Pópulum tibi congregáre non désinis.

10. Jube haec (these) múnera perférri per manus sancti Angeli tui in sublíme altáre tuum.

24. LAUDO, LAUDÁRE, LAUDÁVI, LAUDÁTUM

I praise, to praise, I have praised, praised

STATEMENT

PRINCIPAL PARTS OF VERBS: or BASIC VERB KIT

In English our tenses are formed from three parts of a verb, e.g. give — gave — given. In Latin they are formed from FOUR principal parts e.g. LAUDO — LAUDARE — LAUDAVI — LAUDATUM. The predominant vowel throughout this conjugation is A.

The grouping of Latin verbs into conjugations is based on the predominant VOWEL in each conjugation.

All the tenses studied so far have been derived from the first two PRINCIPAL PARTS.

The PRINCIPAL PARTS of REGULAR, or MODEL, VERBS:

LAUD**O**	LAUDA**RE**	LAUDA**VI**	LAUDA**TUM**
PLACE**O**	PLACE**RE**	PLACUI	PLACI**TUM**
REG**O**	REGE**RE**	REX**I**	REC**TUM**
AUDI**O**	AUDI**RE**	AUDIVI	AUDI**TUM**
ACCIPI**O**	ACCIPE**RE**	ACCEPI	ACCEP**TUM**
gives	confirms	indicates	gives the
all present,	the	perfect	past participle
future and	conjugation	tenses	for perfect
imperfect			tense passive
tenses,			
active and			
passive			

Exercise 24.

Find *in the vocabulary* the principal parts of the following verbs:

1. Adóro
2. Praesto
3. Vídeo
4. Sédeo
5. Déstruo

6. Dico
7. Duco
8. Vénio
9. Séntio
10. Fácio

Some IRREGULAR THIRD CONJUGATION VERBS:

MITTO	MÍTTERE	MISI	MISSUM	— *SEND*
AGO	ÁGERE	EGI	ACTUM	— *DO* or *ACT*
FRANGO	FRÁNGERE	FREGI	FRACTUM	— *BREAK*
RÉDIMO	REDÍMERE	REDÉMI	REDÉMPTUM	— *REDEEM*
RELÍNQUO	RELÍNQUERE	RELÍQUI	RELÍCTUM	— *LEAVE*

Exercise 24a.

Translate:

1. Qui missus es sanáre contrítos corde, miserére nobis (have mercy on us).

2. Agnus redémit oves: Christus ínnocens Patri reconciliávit peccatóres

3. Grátias egit, dedítque discípulis suis, dicens: accípite et bíbite ex eo omnes …

4. Accépit panem et grátias agens, fregit, dedítque discípulis suis, dicens …

5. Quaésumus, Dómine, ut haec múnera fiant (may become) Corpus et Sanguis Christi quod ipse nobis relíquit in foedus aetérnum.

DIES NATIVITATIS DOMINI

25. ET IN SPÍRITUM SANCTUM

And in the Holy Spirit

FOURTH DECLENSION NOUNS: SPIRITUS, spiritus (m) — spirit

Note: These nouns have nom. s. in -US like 'Dominus' but may be distinguished in a vocabulary by the gen. s ending -US: here again the gen. s. serves as a means of identifying the declension.

Nom.	SPIRITUS	— spirit (subject)	SPIRITUS	— spirits (subject)
Voc.	SPIRITUS	— O spirit	SPIRITUS	— O spirits
Acc.	SPIRITUM	— spirit (object)	SPIRITUS	— spirits (object)
Gen.	SPIRITUS	— OF the spirit	SPIRITUUM	— OF spirits
Dat.	SPIRITUI	— TO, FOR the spirit	SPIRITIBUS	— TO, FOR spirits
Abl.	SPIRITU	— BY, WITH, FROM the spirit	SPIRITIBUS	— BY, WITH, FROM spirits

VOCABULARY

VULTUS, vultus (m) — face, countenance
CONSPÉCTUS, conspéctus (m) — sight
ORTUS, ortus (m) — rising

MANUS, manus (f) — hand
DOMUS, domus (f) — house
(n.b.: abl. 'domo' and locative 'domi')
The locative, as its name suggests, indicates location. Thus 'domi' means 'at home', 'Romae' 'at Rome' etc.

NOTE 1: GENU, genus (neuter) — knee

Nom.	GENU	GENUA
Voc.	GENU	GENUA
Acc.	GENU	GENUA
Gen.	GENUS	GENUUM
Dat.	GENU	GENIBUS
Abl.	GENU	GENIBUS

NOTE 2: The name JESUS:

Nom.	JESUS
Voc.	JESU
Acc.	JESUM
Gen.	JESU
Dat.	JESU
Abl.	JESU

Exercise 25.

Translate:

1. In nómine Patris, et Fílii, et Spíritus Sancti. Amen.

2. Glória Patri, et Fílio, et Spirítui Sancto.

3. Dóminus vobíscum: et cum spíritu tuo.

4. Grátia Dómini nostri Jesu Christi et cáritas Dei, et communicátio Sancti Spíritus, sit (be) cum ómnibus (all) vobis.

5. Accépit panem in sanctas ac venerábiles manus suas.

6. Supra (upon) haec múnera propítio ac seréno vultu respícere dignéris.

7. Jube haec múnera perférri in conspéctu divínae majestátis tuae.

8. In nómine Jesu omne genu flectátur (let be bent), caeléstium, terréstrium et infernórum.

9. Unam pétii a Dómino, hanc requíram, ut (that) inhábitem (I may live) in domo Dómini.

10. Ut (so that) a solis ortu usque (until) ad occásum, oblátio munda tibi offerátur (be offered)

26. VISIBÍLIUM OMNIUM ET INVISIBÍLIUM

Of all things, visible and invisible

ADJECTIVES TYPE 2: FIDÉLIS, E — faithful

Adjective Type 1: SANCTUS, A, UM: is derived from noun endings of first and second declensions (see Lesson 13).

Adjective Type 2: is derived from noun endings of third declension nouns type 2 — *finis.*

NOTE: Neuter, nom. voc. and acc. singular — E; abl. singular — I

a)

	S		P	
	m. & f.	*n.*	*m. & f.*	*n.*
Nom.	FIDELIS	FIDELE	FIDELES	FIDELIA
Voc.	FIDELIS	FIDELE	FIDELES	FIDELIA
Acc.	FIDELEM	FIDELE	FIDELES	FIDELIA
Gen.	FIDELIS	FIDELIS	FIDELIUM	FIDELIUM
Dat.	FIDELI	FIDELI	FIDELIBUS	FIDELIBUS
Abl.	FIDELI	FIDELI	FIDELIBUS	FIDELIBUS

b) Some TYPE 2 adjectives have *one ending* for the nominative, whether masc. fem. or neut. e.g. INNOCENS, innocéntis — innocent.

NOTE: Vocabulary gives nom. s. for type a; and nom. s. + *gen.* for type b.

	S		P		
	m. & f.	*n.*	*m.*	*f.*	*n.*
Nom/Voc.	INNOCENS		INNOCENTES		INNOCENTIA
Acc.	INNOCENTEM	INNOCENS	INNOCENTES		INNOCENTIA
Gen.	INNOCENTIS			INNOCENTIUM	
Dat.	INNOCENTI			INNOCENTIBUS	
Abl.	INNOCENTI			INNOCENTIBUS	

Note 1: Present Participles decline like INNOCENS:—

LAUDANS, LAUDÁNTIS	— praising
PLACENS, PLACÉNTIS	— pleasing
REGENS, REGÉNTIS	— ruling
AÚDIENS, AUDIÉNTIS	— hearing
ACCÍPIENS, ACCIPIÉNTIS	— taking

Note 2: Sometimes a pronoun or the word 'person' or 'thing' has to be added to an adjective or participle to fill out the sense:
e.g.　factórem *ómnium visibílium*
maker *of all visible things.*

vox *clamántis* in desérto
the voice *of one crying* in the wilderness

VOCABULARY

OMNIS, omne	— all, every	SÍMILIS, símile	— similar, like
SALUTÁRIS, salutáre	— saving	CAELÉSTIS, caeléste	— heavenly
VISÍBILIS, visíbile	— visible	INVISÍBILIS, invisíbile	— invisible
SUPPLEX, súpplicis	— supplicant	ADMIRÁBILIS, admirábile	— admirable
VENERÁBILIS, venerábile	— venerable	ACCEPTÁBILIS, acceptábile	— acceptable
OMNÍPOTENS, omnipoténtis	— almighty	INCESSÁBILIS, incessábile	— ceaseless
CONSUBSTANTIÁLIS, consubstantiále (+ dative) — consubstantial			

Exercise 26.

Translate:

1. A mórtuis resúrgens, vitam aetérnam nobis donávit.

2. Grátias ágimus tibi ... Dómine Deus, Rex caeléstis, Deus Pater omnípotens.

3. Símili modo postquam (after) cenátum est (supper had been eaten), accípiens et hunc praeclárum cálicem…

4. Oráte, fratres, ut (that) meum ac vestrum sacrifícium acceptábile fiat (may become).

5. Credo in Patrem omnipoténtem, factórem caeli et terrae, visibílium ómnium et invisibílium.

6. Prídie quam paterétur (he suffered) accépit panem in sanctas ac venerábiles manus suas.

7. Ángeli et archángeli proclámant … incessábili voce dicéntes: 'Sanctus' …

8. Meménto (remember + genitive), Dómine, ómnium circumstántium.

9. Communicántes, et memóriam venerántes, in primis gloriósae Vírginis Mariae …

10. Per Jesum Christum, Filium tuum, súpplices rogámus ac pétimus …

27. ET RESURRÉXIT TÉRTIA DIE

And he rose again on the third day

FIFTH DECLENSION NOUNS: DIES, DIÉI (m) — day

There are a few nouns of this type.

NOTE: when a specific day is referred to, e.g. tértia die — on the third day, 'dies' is feminine.

Nom.	**DIES**	— day (subject)	**DIES**	— days (subject)
Voc.	**DIES**	— O day	**DIES**	— O days
Acc.	**DIEM**	— day (object)	**DIES**	— days (object)
Gen.	**DIEI**	— OF a day	**DIERUM**	— OF days
Dat.	**DIEI**	— TO, FOR a day	**DIEBUS**	— TO, FOR days
Abl.	**DIE**	— BY, WITH, FROM a day	**DIEBUS**	— BY, WITH, FROM days

VOCABULARY

FIDES, fídei (f)	— faith	SPES, spei (f)	— hope
RES, rei (f)	— thing, matter	SPÉCIES, speciéi (f)	— appearance

Exercise 27. Translate:

1. Et resurréxit tértia die.

2. Da (give) propítius pacem in diébus nostris.

3. Meménto (remember + gen.) étiam, Dómine, famulórum famularúmque tuárum N. et. N. qui nos praecessérunt cum signo fídei.

4. Ne respícias (do not look on) peccáta nostra, sed fidem Ecclésiae tuae.

5. Exspectántes beátam spem et advéntum Salvatóris nostri Jesu Christi …

6. Surréxit Christus spes mea.

7. O res mirábilis!
   Mandúcat Dóminum
   Pauper, servus et húmilis.

8. Sub divérsis speciébus
   Signis tantum (only) et non rebus
   Latent res exímiae.

9. Una cum fámulo tuo Papa nostro N., et ómnibus orthodóxis et fídei cultóribus …

10. Diésque nostros in tua pace dispónas . . . (may you dispose, order).

28. ADORÁTUR ET CONGLORIFICÁTUR

STATEMENT

He is adored and glorified

THE PASSIVE: *PRESENT, IMPERFECT and FUTURE TENSES*

ACTIVE voice shows the subject doing: God (subject) sent (verb) his Son.

PASSIVE voice shows the subject receiving the action: The Son (subject) is sent (passive verb) by God.

The essential things to grasp are the NEW *Passive Personal Endings.*

— **R**	— **MUR**
— **RIS**	— **MINI**
— **TUR**	— **NTUR**

These simply replace the active personal endings: the root, and the vowels showing the different tenses, remain *exactly* the same.

Look at the PRESENT of LAUD*OR* I am praised:

LAUD*OR*	— I am praised	LAUD*A***MUR**	— we are praised
LAUD*A***RIS**	— you are praised	LAUD*A***MINI**	— you are praised
LAUD*A***TUR**	— he is praised	LAUD*A***NTUR**	— they are praised

The future is: LAUD*ABO***R**, LAUD*ABE***RIS**, LAUD*ABI***TUR**, LAUD*ABI***MUR**, LAUD*ABI***MINI**, LAUD*ABU***NTUR**
The imperfect is: LAUD*ABA***R** etc.
2nd conjugation: PLAC*EO***R**, PLAC*EBO***R**, PLAC*EBA***R**
3rd conjugation: REG*O***R**, REG*A***R** (remember different pattern), REG*EBA***R**
4th conjugation: AUD*IO***R**, AUD*IA***R** (remember different pattern), AUD*IEBA***R**
5th conjugation: ACCIP*IO***R** ACCIP*IA***R** (remember different pattern), ACCIP*IEBA***R**

There are two types of future formation: – B – for 1st and 2nd conjugation verbs and – E – (with – A – for the 1st person singular only) for the others. But ALL verbs, of whichever conjugation, have – BA – in the imperfect.

Exercise 28. Translate:

1. Qui cum Patre et Fílio simul adorátur...

2. Nos qui córpore et sánguine Fílii tui refícimur...

3. Ipse enim, in qua (that which) nocte tradebátur, accépit panem.

4. Aspérges me Dómine hyssópo, et mundábor.

5. Lavábis me, et super nivem dealbábor.

6. Hoc est enim corpus meum, quod (which) pro vobis tradétur.

7. Hic est enim calix sánguinis mei, qui pro vobis et pro multis effundétur.

8. Sed tantum dic verbo et sanábitur ánima mea.

9. Univérsi qui te exspéctant non confundéntur, Dómine.

10. Roráte (drop down dew), caeli désuper, et nubes pluent justum (the just one); aperiétur terra, et germinábit Salvatórem.

29. ET INCARNATUS EST

STATEMENT

And he was made man

The PERFECT PASSIVE is made up of the past participle (see lesson 24, but final M replaced by S) + SUM, ES, EST, etc.

LAUD*ATUS SUM*	— I have been praised	LAUD*ATI SUMUS*	— we have been praised
LAUD*ATUS ES*	etc.	LAUD*ATI ESTIS*	etc.
LAUD*ATUS EST*		LAUD*ATI SUNT*	

You notice that the participle agrees with the subject, because it is a verbal ADJECTIVE and behaves like SANCTUS, A, UM.

Exercise 29.

Translate:

1. Omnes ad quos (to whom) pervénit aqua ista salvi facti sunt.

2. Per quem ómnia facta sunt.

3. Et incarnátus est de Spíritu Sancto ex María Vírgine, et homo factus est.

4. Crucifíxus étiam pro nobis sub Póntio Piláto, passus et sepúltus est.

5. Incarnátus est de Spíritu Sancto, in forma nostrae conditiónis conversátus est.

6. Verbo Dei caeli firmáti sunt.

7. Christus ómnibus discípulis appáruit, et elevátus est in caelum.

8. Laetátus sum (I rejoiced) in his quae (the things which) dicta sunt mihi (= to me).

9. Propítius inténde (listen to, hear) pópulum tuum, super quem (upon whom) invocátum est nomen tuum, Deus.

10. Christus post resurrectiónem suam visus est discípulis maniféstus.

30. EGO SUM PASTOR BONUS
I am the good Shepherd

In the nominative, these personal PRONOUNS are used for emphasis; in the other cases, as well as being used for the meanings given below, they can also be REFLEXIVE.

	S			P	
Nom.	EGO	— I	NOS	— we
Acc.	ME	— me	NOS	— us
Gen.	MEl	— of me (my)	NOSTRI/NOSTRUM	— of us (our)
Dat.	MIHI	— to, for me	NOBIS	— to, for us
Abl.	ME	— by, with, from me	NOBIS	— by, with, from us

	S			P	
Nom.	TU	— you	VOS	— you
Acc.	TE	— you (object)	VOS	— you (object)
Gen.	TUI	— of you (your)	VESTRI/VESTRUM	— of you (your)
Dat.	TIBI	— to, for you	VOBIS	— to, for you
Abl.	TE	— by, with, from you	VOBIS	— by, with, from you

NB. ME + CUM (with) — MECUM — with me
So also TECUM — with you, SECUM — with him
VOBÍSCUM — with you (plural) etc.
SE — himself (reflexive). Et Judas abiens *SE* suspendit. And Judas, going away, hanged *himself.*

Exercise 30.

Translate:

1. Dóminus ('be' understood) vobíscum.

2. Laudámus te, benedícimus te, adorámus te, glorificámus te.

3. Grátias ágimus tibi propter magnam glóriam tuam.

4. Tu solus sanctus, tu solus Dóminus, tu solus Altíssimus.

5. Corpus Christi custódiat (may it preserve) me in vitam aetérnam.

6. Agnus Dei, qui tollis peccáta mundi, miserére (have mercy + dat.) nobis.

7. Ego sum panis vitae.

8. Vias tuas mihi notas fecísti (see facio).

9. Salvátor mundi, salva nos.

10. Ídeo precor (I beseech) beátam Maríam semper Vírginem, omnes ángelos et sanctos, et vos, fratres…

31. HOC EST CORPUS MEUM

This is my body

POSSESSIVE ADJECTIVES.

MEUS, **A**, **UM** — my
TUUS, **A**, **UM** (belonging to one person) — your
SUUS, **A**, **UM** (belonging to the subject) — his, her, its, their
NOST**ER**, NOST**RA**, NOST**RUM** — our
VEST**ER**, VEST**RA**, VEST**RUM** (belonging to several people) — your

NOTE:

EIUS — his, her, its
EORUM — their (fem. EARUM)

Exercise 31.

Translate:

1. Peccávi nimis cogitatióne, verbo, ópere et omissióne, mea culpa, mea culpa, mea máxima culpa.

2. Grátias ágimus tibi propter magnam glóriam tuam.

3. Dóminus exaudívit deprecatiónem eórum.

4. Dóminus sit (be) in corde tuo et in lábiis tuis, ut (so that) digne et competénter annúnties (you may pronounce) Evangélium suum.

5. Suscípiat Dóminus (may the Lord accept) sacrifícium de mánibus tuis, ad laudem et glóriam nóminis sui, ad utilitátem quoque nostram, totiúsque Ecclésiae suae sanctae.

6. Per húius (of this) aquae et vini mystérium eius (i.e. of Christ) efficiámur (may be made) divínitatis consórtes, qui humanitátis nostrae fieri dignátus est (deigned to become) párticeps.

7. Meménto, Dómine, famulórum tuorum, N et N; fides eórum tibi cógnita est, et nota devótio.

8. Hic est enim Calix Sánguinis mei . . . Hoc fácite in meam commemoratiónem.

9. Ne respícias (do not look on) peccáta nostra, sed fidem Ecclésiae tuae.

10. Mortem tuam annuntiámus, Dómine, et tuam resurrectiónem confitémur, donec vénias (until you come).

32. CREDO IN UNUM DEUM

I believe in one God

NUMBERS: One, two, three etc.

The first three numbers are *adjectives,* and agree with the noun that is 'counted'.

	m.	f.	n.	
Nom.	UN**US**	UN**A**	UN**UM**	— one; singular only
Acc.	UN**UM**	UN**AM**	UN**UM**	
Gen.	UN**IUS**	UN**IUS**	UN**IUS**	
Dat.	UN**I**	UN**I**	UN**I**	
Abl.	UN**O**	UN**A**	UN**O**	

Note that UNUS follows SANCTUS (Ch. 13) exactly apart from its gen. and dat. singular – IUS and – I. Similar are NULLUS, SOLUS, TOTUS. Also (but with nom. – er, (e)ra, (e)rum) ALTER and UTER.

Nom.	DUO	DUAE	DUO	— two: plural only
Acc.	DUOS	DUAS	DUO	
Gen.	DUORUM	DUARUM	DUORUM	
Dat.	DUOBUS	DUABUS	DUOBUS	
Abl.	DUOBUS	DUABUS	DUOBUS	

	m/f.	n.	
Nom.	TRES	TRIA	— three: plural only
Acc.	TRES	TRIA	
Gen.	TRIUM	TRIUM	
Dat.	TRIBUS	TRIBUS	
Abl.	TRIBUS	TRIBUS	

Note: PRIMUS, A, UM – first; SECUNDUS, A, UM – second; TÉRTIUS, A, UM — third

These do not decline:

4	QUÁTTUOR	10	DECEM	16	SÉDECIM
5	QUINQUE	11	ÚNDECIM	17	SEPTÉMDECIM
6	SEX	12	DUÓDECIM	18	DUODEVIGÍNTI
7	SEPTEM	13	TRÉDECIM	19	UNDEVIGÍNTI
8	OCTO	14	QUATUÓRDECIM	20	VIGÍNTI
9	NOVEM	15	QUÍNDECIM	100	CENTUM
				1000	MILLE

Not all are used in the Missal, but it seems sensible to include the basic numbers.

Exercise 32.

Translate:

1. Credo in unum Deum . . . Et in unam, sanctam, cathólicam et apostólicam Ecclésiam.

2. Ubi duo vel tres congregáti sunt in nómine meo, ibi sum in médio eórum.

3. Nunc autem manent fides, spes, cáritas, tria haec.

4. Et in unum Dóminum nostrum . . .

5. Quinque vírgines erant fátuae (foolish) et quinque prudéntes.

6. Mille anni ante óculos tuos tamquam (like) dies una.

7. Post dies octo, jánuis clausis, stetit Jesus in médio eórum et dixit: Pax vobis.

8. Ego vos duódecim elégi, et ex vobis unus diábolus est.

9. Et resurréxit tértia die.

10. Quia fílios .. . per sánguinem Fílii tui . . . in unum congregáre voluísti.

33. CONFÍTEOR DEO OMNIPOTÉNTI

I confess to Almighty God

STATEMENT

DEPONENT VERBS

In each conjugation there are verbs that are PASSIVE in shape — but ACTIVE in meaning.

VOCABULARY

1st conjugation:	DIGNOR, dignári, dignátus sum	— to deign
	PRECOR, precári, precátus sum	— to pray
	DÉPRECOR, deprecári, deprecátus sum	— to beseech

2nd conjugation:	MÉREOR, meréri, méritus sum	— to merit
	MISÉREOR, miseréri, misértus sum	— to have pity on
	(+ dative, e.g. miserére (imperative) *nobis* or genitive, e.g. misereátur nostri omnipotens Deus)	

| 3rd conjugation: | LOQUOR, loqui, locútus sum | — to speak |

| 4th conjugation: | LÁRGIOR, largíri, largítus sum | — to give, grant |

| 5th or mixed conjugation: | MÓRIOR, mori, mórtuus sum | — to die |
| | PÁTIOR, pati, passus sum | — to suffer |

NOTE: these verbs have present and future participles active in FORM *and* MEANING.

N.B.: semi-deponents:	AÚDEO, audére, ausus sum	— to dare
	CONFIDO, confídere, confísus sum	— to trust
	FIO, fieri, factus sum	— to be made, become
	GAUDEO, gaudére, gavísus sum	— to rejoice

e.g. Et homo *factus est.* And he was made man.

Look out for PERFECT tenses like *dignátus sum* (compare to *incarnátus est* etc. — see lesson 29).

Look at the *Confíteor* in the Missal. It contains *3* deponent verbs — they look passive (i.e. have characteristic passive endings, see section 28) but have active meanings. Find *I confess, I beseech, may he have mercy...*

Exercise 33. Translate:

1. Confiteor Deo omnipoténti ... quia peccávi nimis.

2. Christus pro nobis mórtuus est atque surréxit.

3. Agnus Dei, qui tollis peccáta mundi, miserére (have mercy) nobis.

4. Crucifíxus étiam pro nobis, passus (see pátior) et sepúltus est.

5. Et in Spiritum Sanctum ... qui (= who) locútus est per prophétas.

6. Confitémur tibi, Pater Sancte, quia magnus es.

7. De tua largitáte accépimus panem ... ex quo (from which) nobis fiet panis vitae.

8. (Christus) humanitátis nostrae dignátus est (see dignor) fieri (infinitive: fio) párticeps.

9. Ipsis, Dómine, et ómnibus in Christo quiescéntibus, locum refrigérii, lucis et pacis ... deprecámur.

10. Per Christum Dóminum nostrum, per quem mundo bona cuncta largíris . . .

34. HIC EST ENIM CALIX . . .

For this is the chalice...

THIS AND THAT: HE, SHE, IT, etc.

THIS

	S.			P.		
nom.	**HIC**	**HAEC**	**HOC**	**HI**	**HAE**	**HAEC**
acc.	**HUNC**	**HANC**	**HOC**	**HOS**	**HAS**	**HAEC**
gen.	**HUIUS**	**HUIUS**	**HUIUS**	**HORUM**	**HARUM**	**HORUM**
dat.	**HUIC**	**HUIC**	**HUIC**	**HIS**	**HIS**	**HIS**
abl.	**HOC**	**HAC**	**HOC**	**HIS**	**HIS**	**HIS**

THAT

nom.	**ILLE**	**ILLA**	**ILLUD**	**ILLI**	**ILLAE**	**ILLA**
acc.	**ILLUM**	**ILLAM**	**ILLUD**	**ILLOS**	**ILLAS**	**ILLA**
gen.	**ILLIUS**	**ILLIUS**	**ILLIUS**	**ILLORUM**	**ILLARUM**	**ILLORUM**
dat.	**ILLI**	**ILLI**	**ILLI**	**ILLIS**	**ILLIS**	**ILLIS**
abl.	**ILLO**	**ILLA**	**ILLO**	**ILLIS**	**ILLIS**	**ILLIS**

	He	She	It	They	They (f)	Those things
nom.	IS	EA	ID	EI	EAE	EA
acc.	EUM	EAM	ID	EOS	EAS	EA
gen.	EIUS	EIUS	EIUS	EORUM	EARUM	EORUM
dat.	EI	EI	EI	EIS	EIS	EIS
abl.	EO	EA	EO	EIS	EIS	EIS

IDEM, EADEM, IDEM — the same, man, woman, thing, adds '-DEM' onto is, ea, id. N.B. acc. eu*n*dem etc.

s.	He himself	She herself	It itself
nom.	IPSE	IPSA	IPSUM
acc.	IPSUM	IPSAM	IPSUM
gen.	IPSIUS	IPSIUS	IPSIUS
dat.	IPSI	IPSI	IPSI
abl.	IPSO	IPSA	IPSO
pl.	IPSI	IPSAE	IPSA
	IPSOS	IPSAS	IPSA
	IPSORUM	IPSARUM	IPSORUM
	IPSIS	IPSIS	IPSIS
	IPSIS	IPSIS	IPSIS

These words are ADJECTIVES when used with a noun, PRONOUNS when they stand alone.

Exercise 34. Translate:

1. Hoc est enim corpus meum.

2. Accípite, bíbite (take, drink) ex eo omnes; hic est enim calix sánguinis mei.

3. Per húius aquae et vini mystérium eius efficiámur (may we be made) divinitátis consórtes.

4. Hábeas et benedícas (accept and bless) haec dona, haec múnera, haec sancta sacrifícia illibáta …

5. Communicántes et noctem sacratíssimam (most holy) celebrántes qua (in which) beáta Maria huic mundo édidit salvatórem …

6. Hanc ígitur oblatiónem servitútis nostrae quaésumus (see quaeso), Dómine, ut placátus accípias (that you will accept).

7. Omnes ad quos pervénit aqua ista salvi facti sunt.

8. Deus ipse est Dóminus; ipse fecit nos, et non ipsi nos.

9. Per ipsum, et cum ipso, et in ipso est tibi … omnis honor et glória.

10. Meménto (be mindful) étiam illórum …

35. QUI TOLLIS PECCATA MUNDI

Who takes away the sins of the world

STATEMENT

RELATIVE PRONOUN 'QUI' — who, which

	s.			p.		
Nom.	QUI	QUAE	QUOD	QUI	QUAE	QUAE
Acc.	QUEM	QUAM	QUOD	QUOS	QUAS	QUAE
Gen.	CUIUS	CUIUS	CUIUS	QUORUM	QUARUM	QUORUM
Dat.	CUI	CUI	CUI	QUIBUS	QUIBUS	QUIBUS
Abl.	QUO	QUA	QUO	QUIBUS	QUIBUS	QUIBUS

Agnus Dei, *qui* tollis peccáta mundi
Lamb of God, (you) who take away the sins of the world …

Per *quem* ómnia facta sunt …
Through *whom* all things were made …

Exercise 35. Translate:

1. Per Christum Dóminum nostrum, qui vivit et regnat in saécula saeculórum.

2. Accépimus panem, quem tibi offérimus … ex quo nobis fiet panis vitae.

3. Accépimus vinum, quod tibi offérimus …

4. Benedícas haec múnera. . quae tibi offérimus.

5. Dóminus réspicit omnes circumstántes … quorum sibi fides cógnita est et nota devótio, pro quibus offérimus …

6. Communicántes et noctem sacratíssimam celebrántes, qua Maria mundo édidit salvatorem.

7. Hoc est enim corpus meum, quod pro vobis tradétur.

8. Hic est enim calix sánguinis mei … qui pro vobis et pro multis effundétur.

9. Pater noster, qui es in caelis.

10. Beáti qui ad cenam Agni vocáti sunt.

NOTE: 'QUI' often serves as a link word to begin a new sentence. You need to supply a noun or pronoun to complete the meaning: Qui sedes ad déxteram Patris … (you) who are seated at the right hand of the Father …

36. OFFÉRIMUS TIBI VINUM ET PANEM

We offer you wine and bread

THREE IRREGULAR VERBS:

1. FERO, FERRE, TULI, LATUM — to carry, bear.

Be able to recognise *compounds* such as:

ÓFFERO, OFFÉRRE, ÓBTULI, OBLÁTUM	— to offer
AÚFERO, AUFÉRRE, ÁBSTULI, ABLÁTUM	— to take away
RÉFERO, REFÉRRE, RÉTULI (or RÉTTULI), RELÁTUM	— to bring

offérimus — we offer

oblátum — thing
obláta — things
} brought (gifts)

2. EO, IRE, IVI, ITUM — to go. Present tense:

EO
IS
IT
IMUS
ITIS
EUNT

Note compounds:

ÓBEO — to die
TRÁNSEO — to move over, to die

3. VOLO, VELLE, VÓLUI — to wish. Present tense:

VOLO
VIS
VULT
VÓLUMUS
VULTIS
VOLUNT

Exercise 36. Translate:

1. De tua largitáte accépimus panem, quem (which) tibi offérimus.

2. Tibi ófferunt hoc sacrifícium laudis, pro se suísque ómnibus …

3. … sacrifícium quod (which) tibi óbtulit summus sacérdos tuus Melchísedech …

4. Jube haec perférri per manus sancti Angeli tui in sublíme altáre tuum.

5. Dómine, haec múnera, quae tibi sacránda (to be sanctified: gerundive, see lesson 43) detúlimus, sanctificáre dignéris (you may think fit).

6. Réspice in ... hóstiam ... cuius immolatióne voluísti placári.

7. Sed et foédera plúries homínibus obtulísti.

8. Meménto etiam illórum, qui obiérunt in pace Christi tui.

9. Laetátus sum (see laetor, dep.) in his quae dicta sunt mihi.

10. Dona Ecclésiae tuae, quibus (in which) non iam aurum, thus et myrrha profértur, sed Jesus Christus.

37. QUIS DEUS PRAETER TE, DÓMINE?

Who is God except you, Lord?

QUESTIONS: questions are usually introduced by an interrogative word.

QUIS? QUID?	— who? what? (declines like QUI) Quid sometimes means 'why?'
QUANDO?	— when?
QUARE?	— why?
QUOT?	— how many?
QUÓMODO?	— how?
UBI?	— where?
UNDE?	— from where?

Exercise 37.

Translate:

1. Quis est iste Rex glóriae?

2. Dic (say) nobis, María, quid vidísti in via?

3. Dóminus illuminátio mea, et salus mea: quem timébo?

4. Dóminus defénsor vitae meae, a quo trepidábo?

5. Ubi est Deus eórum?

6. Quare, Dómine, irásceris in pópulo tuo?

7. Quis ascéndet in montem Dómini?

8. Deus, Deus meus, réspice in me: quare me dereliquísti?

9. Viri Galilaéi, quid admirámini aspiciéntes in caelum?

10. Si iniquitátes observáveris, Dómine: Dómine, quis sustinébit?

38. OPORTÉBAT CHRISTUM PATI

It was fitting for Christ to suffer

STATEMENT

IMPERSONAL VERBS: very rarely, the subject of the verb is 'IT'.

Oportébat Christum pati, et resúrgere a mórtuis tértia die.
IT *was fitting* for Christ to suffer and to rise again from the dead on the third day.

Simili modo, postquam *cenátum est,* accípiens et cálicem . .
In the same way, after supper was ended (IT had been supped), taking also the chalice . . .

Habitáre verbum tuum inter hómines *credebátur.*
It was believed that your Word dwelt among men.

Exercise 38.

1. Nobis non licet interficere quemquam. (to put anyone to death)

2. Te decet hymnus Deus in Sion.

'Good gracious sister ... isn't that rather radical?'

Section B

39. DONA NOBIS PACEM

Grant us peace

IMPERATIVES: Commands, direct pleas.

Active

s.	p.
LAUDA	LAUDATE
PLACE	PLACETE
REGE	REGITE
AUDI	AUDITE
ACCIPE	ACCIPITE

Infinitive	LAUDA + TE
with 're'	PLACE + TE
removed:	etc.
LAUDARE	

Exercise 39

Translate:

1. Agnus Dei, qui tollis peccáta mundi, dona nobis pacem.

2. Réspice, quaésumus, in oblatiónem Ecclésiae tuae.

3. Accípite et manducáte ex hoc omnes: hoc est enim corpus meum.

4, Qui tollis peccáta mundi . . . súscipe deprecatiónem nostram.

5. Salvátor mundi, salva nos.

6. Panem nostrum quotidiánum da nobis hódie.

7. Dimítte nobis débita nostra.

8. Sed líbera nos a malo.

9. Sanctífica, quaésumus, Dómine, haec múnera nostrae servitútis . .

10. Offérte vobis pacem.

Exercise 39a: Turn to the Sequence for Pentecost, *Veni Sancte Spiritus,* in the Missal. There are 16 imperatives: see if you can find them.

40. DIGNÁRE, DÓMINE

Deign, O Lord …

IMPERATIVE PASSIVE

S.		P.	
LAUDARE	— be praised	LAUDAMINI	— be praised etc.
PLACERE	— be pleased	PLACEMINI	
REGERE	— be ruled	REGIMINI	
AUDIRE	— be heard	AUDIEMINI	
ACCIPERE	— be taken	ACCIPIEMINI	

REMEMBER that *deponents* (see lesson 33) *look* passive, *mean* active.

Exercise 40.

Translate:

1. Miserére nostri, Dómine.

2. Dómine, convértere, et éripe ánimam meam.

3. Placáre, Dómine, quaésumus, nostrae précibus humilitátis …

4. Quaérite Dóminum et confirmámini: quaérite faciem eius semper.

5. Dicite pusillanímibus: Confortámini.

6. Jesu, nostri miserére: tu nos pasce, nos tuére …(Lauda Sion).

7. Deus, propitiáre fámulis tuis defúnctis.

8. Nunc ergo, Dómine, ómnium recordáre, pro quibus tibi hanc oblatiónem offérimus.

9. Confitémini Dómino, quóniam bonus (est).

10. Attóllite, portae, cápita vestra, et elevámini, portae aeternáles.

41. DULCIÓRA SUPER MEL

Sweeter than honey

COMPARISON OF ADJECTIVES

Remember the two basic types of adjectives (lessons 13 and 26).

SANCTUS, a, um — good
FIDÉLIS, e — faithful

SANCTUS, SÁNCTIOR, ius	— holier, more holy	SANCTÍSSIMUS, a, um	— holiest, most holy
FIDÉLIS, FIDÉLIOR, ius	— more faithful	FIDELÍSSIMUS, a, um,	— most faithful

Superlatives have same *endings* as SANCTUS, a, um.
Comparatives have same *endings* as FIDELIS, e, *EXCEPT neut. sing. SANCTIUS, and abl. sing. all genders — E instead of — I*

COMPARISON 0F ADVERBS

Comparative adverb has the same form as neut. singular

SANCTIUS — in a more holy manner
FIDÉLIUS — more faithfully

SUPERLATIVE ADVERB

SANCTÍSSIME — in a most holy manner
FIDELÍSSIME — most faithfully

Note: PLUS = more.

Exercise 41.

Translate:

1. Tu solus Dóminus, tu solus altíssimus, Jesu Christe.

2. Dicit Dóminus Petro: Cum esses (when you were) júnior, cingébas te …

3. Communicántes et diem sacratíssimum celebrántes resurrectiónis Dómini nostri Jesu Christi …

4. Libera nos, Dómine, ab ómnibus malis; da propítius pacem in diébus nostris …

5. Justítiae Dómini rectae sunt, et dulcióra super mel et favum.

6. Dómine, cleméntiam tuam fidelíssime implorámus.

7. Alma Redemptóris Mater, Virgo prius ac postérius.

8. Deus qui humánae substántiae dignitátem mirabíliter condidisti et mirabílius reformásti . . .

9. Te ígitur, clementíssime Pater, … súpplices rogámus ac pétimus.

10. Deus, verbo tuo intérius nos páscere dignéris (deign).

42. RESURGÉNDO VITAM REPARÁVIT

By rising again he restored life

GERUND — verbal noun

LAUDA**NDUM**	— (the) praising	PLACE**NDUM**	— (the) pleasing
REGE**NDUM**	— (the) ruling	AUDIE**NDUM**	— (the) hearing
ACCIPIE**NDUM**	— (the) taking		

The GERUND declines like *verbum* (see lesson 10).

1. Not found in *nominative* — INFINITIVE used instead:
   Laboráre est *oráre*   — working is praying.
                              or to work is to pray.

2. Used in *accusative* after a preposition:
   Christus venit non *ad judicándum* sed *ad salvándum.*
   Christ came not *to judge* but *to save.*

3. Used in the *genitive* after some nouns:
   Dedit illis potestátem *curándi* infirmitátes.
   He gave them the power *of curing* diseases.

4. Some verbs take the *dative:*
   Apóstoli studuérunt *evangelizándo.*
   The Apostles gave their attention to *preaching the gospel.*

5. Used to mean 'by' in the *ablative:*
   Celebrándo sacra mystéria sanctificémur.
   By celebrating the sacred mysteries, may we be sanctified.

NOTE: Passives have gerunds active in form and meaning:
          Condítio *moriéndi* — a nature bound *to die.*

Exercise 42.

Translate:

1. Dómine, ad adjuvándum me festína.

2. Qui ad déxteram Patris sedes, ad interpellándum pro nobis: Kýrie eléison.

3. Me vidére est Patrem vidére.

4. Deus, omnipoténtiam tuam parcéndo et miserándo maniféstas.

5. Christus nascéndo (see nascor: dep.) multa gaúdia nobis praéstitit.

6. Mortem nostram moriéndo (see morior, dep.) destrúxit, et vitam resurgéndo reparávit.

7. Nos contrístat certa condítio moriéndi, sed promíssio immortalitátis consolátur.

8. Tribus Dómini Jerúsalem (to Jerusalem) ascendérunt, ad confiténdum nómini tuo, Dómine.

9. Christus pertransívit bene faciéndo et sanándo omnes oppréssos a diábolo.

10. Família tua, Joánnis Praecursóris verba sectándo, ad Christum pervéniat (may it come).

43. AD HOC MAGNUM MYSTÉRIUM CELEBRÁNDUM

To celebrate this great mystery

GERUNDIVE: a 'cousin' of the gerund — this is an *adjective* conveying a sense of purpose or obligation; it *agrees* with its noun, and declines like SANCTUS, a, um;

e.g. Hostiam sacrándam nómini tuo offérimus.
We offer a victim to be made sacred to your name.

Exercise 43.
Translate:

1. Dómine, cum munéribus ad altária veneránda concúrrimus.

2. Deus, tempus ad reparándam puritátem méntium salúbriter statuísti.

3. Vos ad celebrándam sollemnitátem Vírginis Maríae convenisti.

4. Nos quoque, mirándo consórtio, aetérnos reddit.

5. Percéptio córporis tui, Dómine, prosit (may it be of benefit) mihi ad medélam percipiéndam.

6. Concéde, Dómine, pópulum tuum ad incorruptíbilem resurrectiónem glorificándae carnis perveníre.

7. Mors et vita duéllo conflixére (alternative form of 'conflixérunt') mirándo.

8. Da nobis, Dómine, ut proficiámus (that we may come) ad intelligéndum arcánum Christi.

9. Quod in cena Christus gessit,
Faciéndum hoc expréssit,
In sui memóriam.

10. Paulus mágister et doctor géntium vocandárum.

44. ITE, MISSA EST

Go, the Mass is ended

PETITION

IRREGULAR IMPERATIVES: Some of the most common imperatives are irreguiar:

DA	DATE	— give
DIC	DÍCITE	— say
DUC	DÚCITE	— lead
FAC	FÁCITE	— make, grant
FER	FERTE	— bring
I	ITE	— go
ESTO	ESTÓTE	— be
MEMÉNTO	MEMENTÓTE	— remember

e.g. Da robur, fer auxílium — give strength, bring help

Exercise 44.

Translate:

1. Meménto fámuli tui N, quem hódie ex mundo vocásti.

2. Fac nos, quaésumus, Dómine, divinitátis tuae sempitérna fruitióne repléri.

3. Ite, missa est.

4. Dómine, non sum dignus ut intres (that you should enter) sub tectum meum, sed tantum dic verbo (ablative used here) et sanábitur ánima mea.

5. Fac me semper inhaerére mandátis tuis.

6. Propítius esto, Dómine, peccátis nostris.

7. Dic nobis, María, quid vidísti in via?

8. Meménto étiam fratrum nostrórum qui in spe resurrectiónis dormivérunt.

9. Supplicatiónibus nostris, Dómine, adésto (adesse, to be present, near, attentive) propítius.

10. Fac nos, quaésumus, Dómine, caeléstium rerum frequentatióne profícere.

45. ACCÍPIENS ET GRÁTIAS AGENS

…taking, and giving thanks …

PRESENT PARTICIPLES: all participles are verbal *adjectives;* they agree with their nouns.

N.B. declines like INNOCENS, type 2 adjective except that in the Ablative Absolute (see Ch. 44) the ablative singular ends in — E, not — I.

1st. conj.	LAUDANS, LAUDANTIS	— praising, while praising
2nd.conj.	PLACENS, PLACENTIS	— pleasing, while pleasing
3rd. conj.	REGENS etc.	— ruling, while ruling
4th. conj.	AUDIENS	— hearing, while hearing
5th. conj.	ACCIPIENS	— taking, while taking.

NOTE: A participle standing on its own often needs the word 'person', 'people' or 'things' to complete the sense.

Recordáre, Dómine, …hanc oblatiónem offeréntium, et circumstántium.
Be mindful, Lord, of the *people* offering this sacrifice and standing around (your altar).

Exercise 45.

Translate:

1. Justítiae Dómini rectae, laetificántes corda

2. Protéctor in te sperántium, Deus, sine quo nihil est válidum, nihil sanctum …

3. Prope est Dóminus ómnibus vocántibus eum.

4. Da nobis, ut (that), tua praecépta servántes, ad vitam mereámur (we may be worthy) perveníre perpétuam.

5. Communicántes, et diem sacratíssimum celebrántes … et memóriam venerántes …

6. Accípiens et hunc praeclárum cálicem in sanctas ac venerábiles manus suas …

7. Vir erat nómine Job, simplex et rectus et timens Deum.

8. Hymnum glóriae tuae cóncinunt, sine fine dicéntes: Sanctus, sanctus, sanctus …

9. Docéte omnes gentes, baptizántes eos in nómine Patris, et Fílii, et Spíritus Sancti…

10. Sepúlchrum Christi vivéntis, et glóriam vidi resurgéntis.

46. CRUCIFÍXUS ÉTIAM PRO NOBIS

Crucified also for us

PAST AND FUTURE PARTICIPLES

Past Participles: see Lesson 24. Formed from SUPINE — fourth of the 'principal parts'. N.B. PASSIVE in meaning.

1st. conj.	LAUDÁTU**S, a, um**	— having been praised	
2nd. conj.	PLÁCITU**S, a, um**	— having been pleased	
3rd. conj.	RECTU**S, a, um**	— having been ruled	declined like BONUS, a, um
4th. conj.	AUDÍTU**S, a, um**	— having been heard	
5th. conj.	ACCÉPTU**S, a, um**	— having been taken	

Future participles: also formed from SUPINE. Active in meaning.

LAUDATU**RUS, a, um**	— being about to praise	
PLACITU**RUS, a, um**	— being about to please	
RECTU**RUS, a, um**	— being about to rule	declined like BONUS, a, um
AUDITU**RUS, a, um**	— being about to hear	
ACCEPTU**RUS, a, um**	— being about to take	

Exercise 46.

Find the *Credo* in your Missal.

Find and translate the following *past* and *future* participles:

unigénitum	natum	génitum	factum	facta
incarnátus	crucífixus	passus	sepúltus	ventúrus
locútus	ventúri			

47. DIMÍSSIS PECCÁTIS NOSTRIS

our sins having been forgiven

ABLATIVE ABSOLUTE: when a noun is outside the main construction of the sentence and has a participle agreeing with it, both are in the ABLATIVE CASE, e.g.:

Misereátur (may he have mercy) nobis miséricors Dóminus, et, *dimissis peccátis nostris*, perdúcat nos ad vitam aetérnam .

May the merciful Lord have mercy on us and, *our sins having been forgiven,* lead us to eternal life.

Exercise 47.

Translate:

1. Accépit panem, et elevátis óculis in caelum, dedit discípulis suis.

2. Dómine Jesu Christe, cooperánte Spíritu Sancto, per mortem tuam mundum vivificásti.

3. Concéde fidélibus tuis, méntibus purificátis, ad plenitúdinem grátiae filiórum perdúci.

4. Deus, unigénitum Fílium tuum, ómnibus creatúris subjéctis suo (=his) império, óleo exsultatiónis unxísti (see unguo) .

5. Fac nos, Dómine, monte ab inordinátis afféctibus expedíta, rebus perpétuis inhaerére.

6. Post dies octo, jánuis clausis, stetit Jesus in médio discipulórum et dixit: Pax vobis.

7. Misereátur (may he have mercy) mei omnípotens Deus et, dimíssis peccátis meis, perdúcat (may he lead) me ad vitam aetérnam.

8. Sumpto pígnore (pledge) redemptiónis aetérnae, nativitátis mystérium celebrámus.

9. Joánnes Baptísta, fuso sánguine, Christo suprémum testimónium exhibére méruit.

10. Deus, spiritáli purificáto intúitu, glóriam tuam vidére laetémur (may we rejoice).

48. NOLI TIMÉRE

Do not be afraid

NEGATIVE IMPERATIVE

NOLI
NOLÍTE

Exercise 48.

Translate:

1. Veni, Dómine Jesu, et noli tardáre.

2. Bénedic, ánima mea, Dómino, et noli oblivísci omnes retributiónes eius.

3. Mitte manum tuam, et cognósce loca clavórum, et noli esse incrédulus.

4. Nec ego te condemnábo: jam ámplius noli peccáre.

5. Pusillánimes confortámini, et nolíte timére.

'Just a minute – I'll have to look that up.'

Section C

49. SUSCÍPIAT DÓMINUS SACRIFÍCIUM

May the Lord receive the sacrifice

Intercessory prayer is expressed either by the *IMPERATIVE* (see lessons 39, 40, 44 and 48) or by the *JUSSIVE: "may, or let, such and such happen."*

Commands or wishes, expressed by 'may' or 'let' in English, are expressed by the *PRESENT SUBJUNCTIVE* in Latin.

The essential thing to be aware of is the *vowel change* in the connecting letters:

1st conjugation verbs *change* their usual **A** to **E**; all other regular verbs *insert* an **A**; sum, volo and their compounds insert an **I**.
2nd, 3rd, 4th, 5th change to, or add, **A**
ESSE changes to **I**

It is therefore *very important* to know to which *conjugation* the verb belongs: you can do this easily by looking at the PRESENT TENSE and the INFINITIVE, see lessons 1, 2 and 23.

PRESENT SUBJUNCTIVE — ACTIVE

1st	2nd	3rd	4th	5th	Esse	Volo
LAUD*E*M	PLACE*A*M	REG*A*M	AUD*IA*M	ACCIP*IA*M	S*I*M	VEL*I*M
LAUD*E*S	PLACE*A*S	REG*A*S	AUD*IA*S	ACCIP*IA*S	S*I*S	VEL*I*S
LAUD*E*T	PLACE*A*T	REG*A*T	AUD*IA*T	ACCIP*IA*T	S*I*T	VEL*I*T
LAUD*E*MUS	PLACE*A*MUS	REG*A*MUS	AUD*IA*MUS	ACCIP*IA*MUS	S*I*MUS	VEL*I*MUS
LAUD*E*TIS	PLACE*A*TIS	REG*A*TIS	AUD*IA*TIS	ACCIP*IA*TIS	S*I*TIS	VEL*I*TIS
LAUD*E*NT	PLACE*A*NT	REG*A*NT	AUD*IA*NT	ACCIP*IA*NT	S*I*NT	VEL*I*NT

Exercise 49. Translate:

1. Fratres, agnoscámus peccáta nostra.

2. Suscípiat Dóminus sacrifícium de mánibus tuis, ad laudem et glóriam nóminis sui.

3. Pax Dómini sit semper vobíscum.

4. Grátias agámus Dómino Deo nostro.

5. Grátia Dómini nostri Jesu Christi, et cáritas Dei, … sit cum ómnibus vobis.

6. Fiat volúntas tua, sicut in caelo et in terra.

7. A te nunquam me separári permíttas.

8. Dóminus sit in corde tuo et in lábiis tuis.

9. Corpus Christi custódiat me in vitam aetérnam.

10. Benedícat vos omnípotens Deus, Pater, et Fílius, et Spíritus Sanctus.

50. SANCTIFICÉTUR NOMEN TUUM

Hallowed be thy name

WISH

PRESENT SUBJUNCTIVE PASSIVE: again the *essential* thing to spot is the VOWEL CHANGE, as shown above.

REMEMBER the passive- personal endings:

— R	— MUR
— RIS	— MINI
— TUR	— NTUR

LAUD*E*R	PLAC*EA*R	REG*A*R	AUD*IA*R	ACCIP*IA*R
LAUD*E*RIS	PLAC*EA*RIS	REG*A*RIS	AUD*IA*RIS	ACCIP*IA*RIS
LAUD*E*TUR	PLAC*EA*TUR	REG*A*TUR	AUD*IA*TUR	ACCIP*IA*TUR
LAUD*E*MUR	PLAC*EA*MUR	REG*A*MUR	AUD*IA*MUR	ACCIP*IA*MUR
LAUD*E*MINI	PLAC*EA*MINI	REG*A*MINI	AUD*IA*MINI	ACCIP*IA*MINI
LAUD*E*NTUR	PLAC*EA*NTUR	REG*A*NTUR	AUD*IA*NTUR	ACCIP*IA*NTUR

REMEMBER DEPONENT verbs, which *look* passive but *mean* active.

Exercise 50.

Translate:

1. In te Dómine sperávi: non confúndar in aetérnum.

2. Per evangélica dicta deleántur nostra delícta.

3. (Ecclésiam tuam) pacificáre, custodíre, adunáre et régere dignéris toto orbe terrárum.

4. Per húius aquae et vini mystérium eius efficiámur divinitátis consórtes.

5. Sanctificétur nomen tuum; advéniat regnum tuum.

6. In spíritu humilitátis et in ánimo contríto suscipiámur a te, Dómine.

7. Omni benedictióne caelésti et grátia repleámur.

8. Unum corpus et unus spíritus inveniámur in Christo.

9. Dómine, non confúndar, quóniam invocávi te.

10. Per passiónem eius et crucem ad resurrectiónis glóriam perducámur.

51. NE NOS INDÚCAS

Lead us not …

NEGATIVE SUBJUNCTIVE: preceded by NE. For the subjunctive see lesson 49.

Exercise 51.

Translate:

1. Ne respícias peccáta nostra, sed fidem Ecclésiae tuae.

2. Et ne nos indúcas in tentatiónem.

3. Ánimas paúperum tuórum ne obliviscáris in finem.

4. Líbera eas de ore leónis, ne absórbeat eas tártarus, ne cadant in obscúrum.

5. Ne avértas fáciem tuam a me.

52. ROGÁMUS UT

We beseech that

INDIRECT COMMAND/PETITION: many prayers strengthen a wish with a verb of strong entreaty, e.g.

Rogámus ut ad vitam aetérnam mereámur pervveníre.

We beseech that we may be worthy to come to eternal life.

Remember too that many verbs of entreaty are followed by an INFINITIVE.

Tríbue nobis toto corde tibi servíre.

Grant that we may serve you with all our heart.

NOTE: UT, UTI = that.

Be on the lookout for the following as key words (especially in Eucharistic prayers, opening prayers and prayers after Communion):

> FAC
> DA
> PRAESTA
> CONCÉDE
> TRÍBUE
> ORÁTE
> QUAÉSUMUS
> ROGÁMUS
> PÉTIMUS
> PRECOR
> DEPRECÁMUR
> EXORÁMUS

Exercise 52.

Translate:

1. Hanc igitur oblatiónem servitútis nostrae, quaésumus, Dómine, ut placátus accípias.

2. Súpplices rogámus ac pétimus uti accépta hábeas et benedícas haec dona.

3. Tríbue, quaésumus, ut beátam Maríam pro nobis intercédere sentiámus.

4. Oráte, fratres, ut meum ac vestrum sacrifícium acceptábile fiat apud Deum Patrem omnipoténtem.

5. Ídeo precor beátam Maríam semper vírginem, omnes ángelos et sanctos, et vos fratres, oráre pro me ad Dóminum Deum nostrum.

6. Ipsis, Dómine, et ómnibus in Christo quiescéntibus, locum refrigérii, lucis et pacis ut indúlgeas deprecámur.

7. Fac nos, omnípotens Deus, sanctis gaúdiis exsultáre, et pia gratiárum actióne ascensiónis Fílii tui laetári.

8. Praesta ut in nobis quae sunt bona nútrias, et quae sunt nutríta custódias.

9. Concéde ut, húius participatióne mystérii, dóceas nos caeléstibus inhaerére.

10. Unam (one thing) petívi a Dómino, hanc (agrees with unam) requíram, ut inhábitem in domo Dómini.

Exercise 52a.

Look at the opening prayers for the following feasts: and pick out the KEY words, i.e. the imperatives:

Christ the King.
Holy Trinity.
Corpus Christi.
Vigil of St John the Baptist (23rd June).

53. FIAT LUX

Let there be light

WISH

FIO, FÍERI, FACTUS SUM — I become *or* am made, conjugates like ACCIPIO. Looks active (except for the infinitive) until the perfect, then looks passive. Two parts which occur most often in the Missal are:

Subjunctive: FIAT — let him, it, become or be done
FIANT — let them become

Infinitive: FÍERI — to become

POSSUM, POSSÉ, PÓTUI — I am able, I can.
A curious compound of SUM with prefix either POT or POS

Present

POSSUM	POSSUMUS
POTES	POTESTIS
POTEST	POSSUNT

NOTE especially present subjunctive:

POSSIM	POSSIMUS
POSSIS	POSSITIS
POSSIT	POSSINT

Exercise 53.

Translate:

1. Sic fiat sacrifícium nostrum in conspéctu tuo hódie ut pláceat tibi.

2. Quantum potes, tantum aude,
   Quia major omni laude,
   Nec laudáre súfficis.

3. Fiat volúntas tua, sicut in caelo et in terra.

4. Concéde fámulis tuis ut te conditórem et redemptórem possint perpétuo contemplári.

5. Haec ergo dona, quaésumus, sanctífica, ut nobis corpus et sanguis fiant dilectíssimi Fílii tui.

6. Quaésumus ut possint ad aetérnam vitam perveníre felíces.

7. Haec commíxtio Córporis et Sánguinis Dómini nostri Jesu Christi fiat accipiéntibus nobis in vitam aetérnam.

8. Praesta, Dómine, ut tibi mundo corde appropinquáre possímus.

9. Múnera quae offérimus nobis fiant praémium redemptiónis aetérnae tuae.

10. Da nobis, Dómine, eius divinitátis esse consórtes, qui humanitátis nostrae fieri dignátus est párticeps.

'Don't look now, Father ... but I think he's learning his irregular verbs!'

This section looks at clauses which express ideas that are *additional* to the main one: they tell us why, when, if, such and such were to happen.

54. UT NOBIS FIANT CORPUS ET SANGUIS

So that they may become for us the body and blood

PURPOSE CLAUSES: prayers often express a purpose.

UT, UTI = in order to, so that

NE
UT NON } = lest, so that … not

Sanctífica haec dona *ut nobis fiant corpus et sanguis.*
Bless these gifts *so that they may become for us the body and blood.*

When the *main verb* is in the *past* tense, it is followed by the IMPERFECT SUBJUNCTIVE. This is easily recognised: the personal endings, active or passive, are simply added to the present infinitive.

Active	*Passive*	*Verb 'to be'*	*Verb 'to wish'*
LAUDAREM	LAUDARER	ESSEM	VELLEM
LAUDARES	LAUDARERIS	ESSES	VELLES
LAUDARET	LAUDARETUR	ESSET	VELLET
LAUDAREMUS	LAUDAREMUR	ESSEMUS	VELLEMUS
LAUDARETIS	LAUDAREMINI	ESSETIS	VELLETIS
LAUDARENT	LAUDARENTUR	ESSENT etc.	VELLENT

Exercise 54.

Translate:

1. Dóminus sit in corde tuo et in lábiis tuis, ut digne et competénter annúnties Evangélium suum.

2. Recordáre (takes genitive), Dómine, Ecclésiae tuae, ut eam in caritáte perfícias.

3. Deus illúminet vultum suum super nos, ut cognoscámus in terra viam suam.

4. Et in mánibus tollent te, ne forte offéndas ad lápidem pedem tuum.

5. Fílius hóminis venit, ut daret ánimam suam in redemptiónem pro multis.

6. Deus, Fílium tuum óleo exsultatiónis unxísti ut regnum tráderet imménsae majestáti tuae.

7. Ómnibus subvenísti (takes dative) ut te quaérentes invenírent.

8. Dóminus in mortem se trádidit ut mortem destrúeret et vitam renováret.

9. Ascéndant ad te, Dómine, preces nostrae, ut tuis sacraméntis aptémur.

10. Álium Paráclitum dabit vobis, ut máneat vobíscum in aetérnum.

55. QUIA DE TUA LARGITÁTE ACCÉPIMUS

EXTRAS

Because we have received from your bounty

QUIA
QUÓNIAM } = because (+ indicative)

'Because' clauses have their verb in the indicative.

Exercise 55.

Translate:

1. Benedíctus es, Dómine, Deus univérsi, quia de tua largitáte accépimus panem.

2. Cálicem offérimus grátias agéntes quia nos dignos habuísti (you have held) astáre coram te et tibi ministráre.

3. Vere sanctus es, Dómine, quia per Fílium tuum, Spíritus Sancti operánte virtúte, vivíficas et sanctíficas univérsa.

4. Grátias ágimus tibi, quóniam tu solus sanctus, tu solus Dóminus, tu solus altíssimus, Jesu Christe.

5. Vere dignum et justum est tibi grátias ágere, quia in Christo salútis nostrae mystérium hódie revelavísti.

6. Confitémur tibi, Pater sancte, quia magnus es, et ómnia ópera tua in sapiéntia et caritáte fecísti.

7. Laeténtur caeli et exsúltet terra ante fáciem Dómini, quóniam véniet.

8. Veníte gentes, et adoráte Dóminum: quia hódie descéndit lux magna super terram.

9. Et concupíscet rex spéciem tuam, quóniam ipse est dóminus tuus, et adóra eum.

10. Felix namque es, sacra Virgo María, et omni laude (dignus takes the ablative) digníssima: quia ex te ortus est sol justítiae, Christus Deus noster.

56. CUM HORA VENÍSSET

When the hour had come

EXTRAS

TEMPORAL CLAUSES

POSTQUAM	— after	
CUM, UBI, QUANDO	— when	
ÁNTEQUAM, PRIÚSQUAM	— before	+ indicative
DONEC	— until	OR
DUM	— while	subjunctive
QUOTIESCÚMQUE	— whenever	

'CUM' = when + PLUPERFECT SUBJUNCTIVE in the past:

PLUPERFECT SUBJUNCTIVE

Active: Passive:

Perfect Stem + special endings.   Past Part. + imperf. subj. of ESSE

LAUDA*VISSE*M	LAUDA*VISSE*MUS	LAUDAT*US*	ESSEM	LAUDATI	ESSEMUS
LAUDA*VISSE*S	LAUDA*VISSE*TIS	LAUDAT*US*	ESSES	LAUDATI	ESSETIS
LAUDA*VISSE*T	LAUDA*VISSE*NT	LAUDAT*US*	ESSET	LAUDATI	ESSENT

Haec *cum dixísset* Jesus, egréssus est.
When Jesus *had said* these things, he went out.

Exercise 56.

Translate:

1. Símili modo, postquam cenátum est (after supper had been eaten), accípiens et hunc praeclárum cálicem … benedíxit.

2. Dixit Dóminus Petro: cum esses júnior, cingébas te et ambulábas ubi volébas.

3. Quotiescúmque manducámus panem hunc et cálicem bíbimus, mortem tuam annuntiámus, Dómine, donec vénias.

4. Cum gustavísset architriclínus aquam vinum factam, dixit sponso …

5. Dum médium siléntium tenérent ómnia, omnípotens sermo tuus de caelis a regálibus sédibus venit.

6. Mortem tuam annuntiámus, Dómine, et tuam resurrectiónem confitémur, donec vénias.

7. Priúsquam te formárem in útero, novi te; et ántequam exíres de ventre, sanctificávi te.

8. Concéde ut, qui mórtuus in Christo, vivat in ipso, quando mórtuos suscitábit in carne de terra.

9. Qui cum passióni voluntárie traderétur, accépit panem et, grátias agens, fregit.

10. Priúsquam te Phílippus vocáret, cum esses sub ficu (fig tree) vidi te.

57. POSTQUAM AUTEM RESURRÉXERO

But after I shall have risen again

| EXTRAS |

You will often find the FUTURE PERFECT used after 'CUM' and 'POSTQUAM' meaning 'when'.

Postquam autem *resurréxero,* praecédam vos in Galilaéam.
But after *I have risen again* ('shall have risen again') I shall go before you into Galilee.

The Future Perfect is simply the perfect stem + ero, eris, erit, erimus, eritis, erunt (future of ESSE q.v. lesson 15):

LAUDAV**ERO**
PLACU**ERO**
REX**ERO**   etc.

Exercise 57.
Translate:

1. Cum ergo vénerit Spíritus Sanctus nobis annuntiábit ómnia.

2. Cum secúndo (a second time) vénerit in glória suae majestátis, manifésto múnera capiémus.

3. Si quis (anyone) audíverit verba mea et non custodíverit, ego non júdico eum.

4. De quacúmque tribulatióne clamáverint ad me, exaúdiam eos.

5. Beátus servus qui, cum vénerit Dóminus, invénerit vigilántem.

6. Ubicúmque fúerit corpus, illuc (to that place) congregabúntur et áquilae.

7. Cum Christus apparúerit, similes ei érimus, quóniam vidébimus eum sicúti est.

8. Cum autem senúeris, exténdes manus tuas, et álius te cinget, et ducet quo non vis.

9. Panis, quem ego dédero, caro mea est pro saéculi vita.

10. Cum íterum ad Patrem meum ascéndero Paráclitum vobis mittam.

58. TÉRTIA DIE

On the third day

1   TIME

a)   a point in time is expressed by the ABLATIVE case:
Et resurréxit TÉRTIA DIE
And he rose again on the third day.
NOTE: DIES — day, is feminine when a *specific* day is named.

b) revise prepositions:

DE + abl.	— from
IN + abl.	— on, in
IN + acc.	— into
ANTE + acc.	— before
POST + acc.	— after
USQUE AD/IN + acc.	— until
AD + acc.	— to, into

NOTE: HÓDIE (adv.) — hoc die : abl. case — today.

2. PLACE

Revise prepositions:

AB + abl.	— from
IN + abl.	— in, at
IN + acc.	— to
AD + acc.	— near, at
SECUS + acc.	— by, beside

Exercise 58.

Translate:

1. Da propítius pacem in diébus nostris.

2. Descéndit de caelis … et ascéndit in caelum, sedet ad déxteram Patris.

3. A solis ortu usque ad occásum oblátio munda offerátur nómini tuo.

4. Glória in excélsis Deo, et in terra pax homínibus bonae voluntátis.

5. Vere dignum et justum est … te confitéri et in hac potíssimum (especially) die gloriósius praedicáre, cum Pascha nostrum immolátus est Christus.

6. Post dies octo, jánuis clausis, stetit Jesus in médio discipulórum.

7. Corpus Christi custódiat me in vitam aetérnam.

8. Unde et mémores (+ genitive), Dómine … tam beátae passiónis, necnon et ab ínferis resurrectiónis, sed et in caelos gloriósae ascensiónis Fílii tui Jesu Chrísti …

9. Et in Jesum Christum … ex Patre natum ante ómnia saécula.

10. Deus, Deus meus, ad te de luce vígilo.

59. ALTER CRUCE, ALTER GLÁDIO

One by the cross, the other by the sword

CORRELATIVES: 'POINTERS': throughout the Missal you will notice 'pointer' words: one occurs in the first half of the sentence, its link word in the second half.

They connect: single words
                 phrases
                 clauses
                 sentences.

Hic princeps fídei confiténdae, *ille* intelligéndae clarus assértor.
The former (St Peter) was the prince of confessors of the faith, *the latter* (St Paul) its illustrious teacher.

Exercise 59.

Translate:

1. Petrus clave, Paulus verbo nos in pátriam indúcant, ad quam meruérunt, *alter* cruce, *alter* gládio, felíciter perveníre.

2. *Eo* pervéniat humílitas gregis *quo* procéssit fortitúdo pastóris.

3. Nobis próvides de ipsa mortalitáte remédium, et pérditos quosque (whoever) *unde* períerant *inde* salvásti.

4. *Qui* cum nascéndo (at his birth) multa gaúdia praestitísset, *ipse* solus ómnium prophetárum agnum redemptiónis osténdit.

5. ...*illuc* confídimus, sua membra, nos súbsequi *quo* ipse caput nostrum praecéssit.

60. SIC DEUS MUNDUM DILÉXIT UT
God so loved the world that

RESULT CLAUSES

Sic enim Deus diléxit mundum *ut* Filium suum unigénitum daret.
God *so* loved the world *that* he gave his only-begotten Son.

SIC
ITA ⎫ — so, in such a way
UT ⎬ — (so) that

followed by the verb in the SUBJUNCTIVE, either present or imperfect.

Sic lúceat lux vestra coram homínibus *ut* vídeant ópera vestra bona.
May your light *so* shine among men *that* they may see your good works.

Jesus coepit *ita* praedicáre *ut* iam non posset maniféste introíre in civitátem.
Jesus began to preach *in such a way that* he was not now able to go openly into the city.

Exercise 60.

Translate:

1. Sic convertímini ut deleántur peccáta vestra.

2. Sic ovis ad occisiónem ductus est ut non aperíret os suum.

3. Sic bonis transeúntibus nunc utámur (utor here takes the ablative) ut iam possímus inhaerére mansúris (= those things which last) .

4. Deus, sic mundum dilexísti ut nobis Salvatórem mítteres.

5. Sic fiat sacrifícium nostrum in conspéctu tuo hódie, ut pláceat tibi.

61. QUANTUM POTES, TANTUM AUDE
As much as you can, that much dare

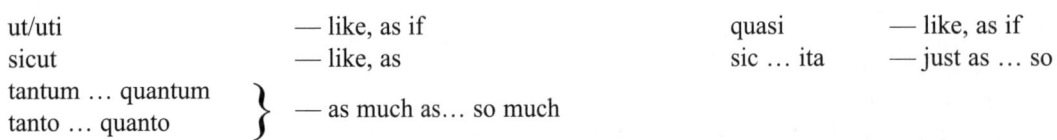

COMPARATIVE CLAUSES: sometimes a clause or phrase compares one action to another, e.g.

Quemádmodum vidístis eum ascendéntem in caelum *ita* véniet.
As you have seen him going up into heaven, *so* he will come again.

Comparative words:

ut/uti	— like, as if	quasi	— like, as if
sicut	— like, as	sic ... ita	— just as ... so
tantum ... quantum tanto ... quanto	⎬ — as much as... so much		

Exercise 61.

Translate:

1. Dimítte nobis débita nostra, sicut et nos dimíttimus debitóribus nostris.

2. Dignéris respícere supra panem et cálicem, sícuti accépta habére dignátus es múnera púeri tui justi Abel.

3. Justus ut palma florébit: sicut cedrus quae in Líbano est, multiplicábitur.

4. Concédat ut sicut Christus post resurrectiónem suam visus est, ita vobis pro aeternitáte placátus appáreat.

5. Quantum potes, tantum aude,
   Quia major omni laude,
   Nec laudáre súfficis.

6. Sumit unus, sumunt mille,
   Quantum isti, tantum ille.
   Nec sumptus consúmitur.

7. Fiat volúntas tua, sicut in caelo, et in terra.

8. Qui confídunt in Dómino, sicut mons Sion ('sunt' understood): non commovébitur in aetérnum qui hábitat in Jerúsalem.

9. Quantum sumus formidántes (full of dread) de nostro mérito, tantum de tua benignitáte confídimus.

10. Tanto devótius proficiámus, quanto magis dies salutífera accédit (approaches).

62. SI ÁMBULEM IN MÉDIO UMBRAE MORTIS

Even if I walk in the midst of the shadow of death

EXTRAS

CONDITIONAL CLAUSES

Si — if;   Etsi — even if;   Nisi — if not, unless (sometimes 'si non')

In many sentences 'if' almost means 'when'; then both verbs are in the *indicative,* often *future* or *future perfect.*
When the condition of the 'if' clause *really* means 'if', and is expressed in English by 'were to', 'should' etc., the verb is in the *subjunctive.*

Si *ámbulem* in médio umbrae mortis, non *timébo* mala.
If I *should walk* in the midst of the shadow of death, I *will fear* no evil.

Exercise 62.

Translate:

1. Qui credit in me, si mórtuus fúerit, vivet.

2. Si dilígitis me, mandáta mea serváte, dicit Dóminus.

3. Si vis, potes me mundáre.

4. Si quis audíverit vocem meam, et aperúerit mihi jánuam, intrábo ad illum.

5. Nisi granum fruménti cadens in terram mórtuum fúerit, ipsum solum manet.

6. Si autem mórtuum fúerit, multum fructum affert (see fero, lesson 35).

7. Pater, si non potest hic calix transíre nisi bibam illum, fiat volúntas tua.

8. Si non esset malefáctor, non tibi tradidissémus eum.

9. Quis potest dimíttere peccáta, nisi solus Deus?

10. Si quis manducáverit ex hoc pane, vivet in aetérnum.

63. SCIMUS CHRISTUM SURREXÍSSE

We know that Christ has risen

INDIRECT SPEECH

Direct Speech gives the actual words of the speaker:

Dixi: "Tu es Deus meus, in mánibus tuis témpora mea."

I said: "You are my God, my life (is) in your hands."

Indirect Speech REPORTS what someone is saying, thinking, knowing etc. in a clause:

Sciant gentes *quia* nomen tuum est Deus.

May the people know *that* your name is God.

Sometimes the *subject* of the report is put in the *accusative* case and the verb is in the *infinitive.*

Vox Patris intónuit *illum esse* filium suum diléctum.

The voice of the Father thundered *that this was* his beloved Son.

The infinitive reflects the tense used by the speaker or thinker *at the time,* so remember the different tenses of the INFINITIVE:

PRESENT   PAST

Act.	Laudáre	— to praise		Act.	Laudavísse	— to have praised
Pass.	Laudári	— to be praised		Pass.	Laudátus esse	— to have been praised

FUTURE

Act.   Laudatúrus esse — to be about to praise.

Exercise 63.

Translate:

1. Scimus Christum surrexísse a mórtuis vere.

2. Confiteor Deo omnipoténti, quia peccávi nimís.

3. Nos habuísti (you have thought) dignos esse astáre coram te.

4. Dómine, crédidi quia tu es Christus Fílius Dei vivi, qui in hunc mundum venisti.

5. Nesciebátis quia in his (these matters) quae Patris mei sunt opórtet me (it is my duty) esse?

6. Joánnes Baptísta Christum affutúrum (esse) cécinit et adésse monstrávit.

7. Hódie sciétis quia véniet Dóminus, et salvábit nos.

8. Agnoscámus Christum servum tuum mitti ad evangelizándum paupéribus.

9. Respónsum accépit Simeon a Spiritu Sancto, non se visúrum (esse) mortem nisi (unless/until) vidéret Christum Dóminum.

10. Per vocem de caelo habitáre Verbum tuum inter hómines crédimus.

'... audiveruntne missam latine secundum decretum'

Section E

PROPER NOUNS

64. AVE MARÍA

Hail Mary

Proper nouns are the particular names of people (e.g. Peter), places (Jerusalem) and nations (Israel), as well as special days and occasions (Easter Sunday, the Passover). In Latin most of these decline like nouns of the 1st, 2nd and 3rd declensions. In this section we will look at these regular nouns. See also vocabulary of proper nouns and adjectives on p114.

lst declension: María, Maríae (f) — Mary
Lúcia, Lúciae (f) — Lucy
Baptísta, Baptístae (m) — the Baptist
Some masculine nouns of the 1st declension have the ending -AS in the nominative but otherwise are declined like *ecclésia*.
Isaías, Isaíae (m) — Isaiah
Thomas, Thomae (m) — Thomas
Andréas, Andréae (m) — Andrew

2nd declension: Christus, Christi (m) — Christ
Petrus, Petri (m) — Peter
Paulus, Pauli (m) — Paul

3rd declension: Joánnes, Joánnis (m) — John
Míchael, Michaélis (m) — Michael
Simon, Simónis (m) — Simon

VOCABULARY

Jordánis, Jordánis (m) — the Jordan
Póntius Pilátus, Póntii Piláti (m) — Pontius Pilate
Samaritána, Samaritánae (f) — Samaritan woman
Lázarus, Lázari (m) — Lazarus
Galilaéa, Galilaéae (f) — Galilee

Exercise 64.

Translate:

1. Ídeo precor beátam Maríam semper vírginem.

2. Christus a Joánne in Jordáne baptizátur.

3. Crucifíxus étiam pro nobis sub Póntio Piláto.

4. Dixit Dóminus Samaritánae: Da mihi bíbere.

5. Dóminus secus mare Galiléae vidit duos fratres Petrum et Andréam, et vocávit eos.

6. Et incarnátus est de Spíritu Sancto, ex María Vírgine.

7. Simon Joánnis (= son of John), díligis me?

8. Vidit Dóminus flentes soróres Lázari ad monuméntum; clamábat: Lázare, veni foras.

9. Sígnifer sanctus Míchael repraeséntet eos in lucem sanctam.

10. Ave María, grátia plena, Dóminus tecum.

65. DÓMINE JESU CHRISTE

O Lord Jesus Christ

THREE IRREGULAR NOUNS

1. The Holy Name of *Jesus* declines as follows:

> Nom. JESUS
> Voc. JESU
> Acc. JESUM
> Gen. JESU
> Dat. JESU
> Abl. JESU

2. The name *Ábraham* is sometimes not declined, but often has the genitive and dative *Ábrahae*.

3. The name *Jerúsalem* is found in two forms: *Jerosólyma* (f), and *Jerúsalem* (n) which is not declined.

4. Place names occuring in the acusative sometimes do so with a preposition, sometimes without, as in No. 5 below, where 'Jerosólymam' also means 'to Jerusalem.'

Exercise 65.

Translate:

1. Dómine Jesu Christe, Fili Dei vivi, miserére nobis.

2. Venit Dóminus in civitátem Jerúsalem.

3. Dixit Andréas Simóni fratri suo: Invénimus Messíam, qui dícitur Christus; et addúxit eum ad Jesum.

4. Prómissum Ábrahae dedísti et sémini eius in saécula.

5. Erant in via ascendéntes Jerosólymam.

6. Dixit Jesus discípulis suis: Data est mihi omnis potéstas in caelo et in terra.

7. Dignátus es accípere sacrifícium Patriárchae nostri Ábrahae.

8. Corpus et Sanguis Jesu Christi.

9. Per Jesum Christum Dóminum nostrum.

10. Jerúsalem, Jerúsalem. convértere ad Dóminum Deum tuum.

66. SACÉRDOS TUUS MELCHÍSEDECH

Your priest Melchisedech

HEBREW NAMES

Many Hebrew names are used in Latin as indeclinable nouns. Mostly these are individual personal names, such as *Ísaac, Abel* and *Joseph,* but notice *Séraphim* and *Chérubim,* which are Hebrew masculine plurals, and *Sábaoth,* which is a feminine plural, 'great armies'.

As in English, with indeclinable nouns you use the rest of the sentence to decide which case they are in:
Hosánna Fílio David = Hosanna to the Son of David (genitive).
Laetáre, Jerúsalem = Rejoice, Jerusalem (vocative).
Dóminus Jacob vocávit = The Lord called Jacob (accusative).

A list of some indeclinable proper nouns (they are the same in English, except where shown):

Abel	Joseph
Bénjamin	Manásse (= Manasses)
Chérubim	Melchísedech
Emmánuel	Saba (= Seba, Sheba)
Éphraim	Satan
Isráel	Sion
Ísaac	Tharsis (= Tarshish)
Jesse	

Exercise 66.

Translate:

1. Avertísti, Dómine, captivitátem Jacob.

2. Ecce virgo concípiet et páriet fílium: et vocábitur nomen eius Emmánuel.

3. Tibi óbtulit sacrifícium summus sacérdos tuus Melchísedech.

4. Benedíctus Dóminus Deus Ísrael.

5. Reges Tharsis et ínsulae múnera ófferent: reges Árabum (= of the Arabians) et Saba dona addúcent.

6. Qui regis Ísrael inténde: qui dedúcis velut ovem Joseph: qui sedes super Chérubim, appáre coram Éphraim, Bénjamin et Manásse.

7. Haec est generátio quaeréntium (= of those who seek) fáciem Dei Jacob.

8. Lauda Sion Salvatórem.

9. Virga (n.b. not virgo) Jesse flóruit.

10. Vir erat in terra nómine Job; Satan Deum pétiit ut tentáret eum.

"Turn the altar round, bring me my Missale Romanum *and GET YOUR HAIR CUT!"*

ANSWERS

Exercise A

1. Noun. pron. verb. adj. adv. conj. adj. noun. adv. verb. pron. noun.
2. Pron. verb. adj. (article) noun. conj. prep. noun. prep. noun. adj. (article) adj. noun. verb.
3. Noun. prep. possessive adj. noun. conj. noun. pron. verb. pron. adj.
4. Pron. verb. pron. noun. possessive adj. noun. pron. verb. pron.
5. Pron. relative pron. verb. prep. pron. verb. adv. verb. adj.

Exercise B

1. (I) am the true vine.
2. (You) teach us how to live in this passing world.
3. (He) proclaimed the good news of Salvation.
4. (The wise men) followed the star.
5. With shouts of joy (God) goes up.

Exercise C

1. who proceeds from the Father and the Son.
2. as we wait in joyful hope for the coming of our Saviour.
3. that we might live no longer for ourselves.
4. because you alone are God, living and true.
5. for he has worked wonders.

Exercise D

1. they are; we pray; they go; hearts; brothers; sinners.
2. I confessed; we believed; they became.
3. me; us; whom.

Exercise E

1. nominative
2. vocative
3. accusative
4. genitive
5. dative
6. ablative

Exercise 1

1. We praise you. 1st.
2. We adore you. 1st.
3. Who with you lives and reigns for ever and ever. 1st.
4. Who sit at the right hand of the Father. 2nd.
5. O good king, to whom all good things are pleasing. 2nd.
6. Who live and reign with God the Father. 1st.
7. We hope in you, O Lord. 1st.
8. We glorify you. 1st.
9. And I await the resurrection of the dead. 1st.
10. We ask and beseech. 1st.

Exercise 2

1. We bless you. 3rd.
2. Who with you lives and reigns for ever and ever. 3rd, 1st.

3. Today Christ rises again. 3rd.

4. Blessed is he who comes in the name of the Lord. 4th.

5. We are aware without distinction. 4th.

6. You grant graciously to your faithful people. 3rd.

7. I tell my works to the king. 3rd.

8. You look at the faith of your Church. 5th.

9. The Lord our God looks at lowly things. 5th.

10. The body of Christ preserves me to eternal life. 4th.

Exercise 3

1.	Church, fem.	nom.	voc.	abl.	s.
2.	Mercy, fem.	nom.	voc.	abl.	s.
3.	Fault, fem.	nom,	voc.	abl.	s.
4.	Water, fem.	acc.			s.
5.	Grace, fem.	nom.	voc.	abl.	s.
6.	Life, fem.	acc.			s.
7.	Soul, fem.	acc.			s.
8.	Earth, fem.	gen.	dat.		s.
9.	Church, fem.	gen.	dat.		s.
10.	Life, fem.	gen.	dat.		s.

Exercise 4

1.	Gates, fem.	nom.	voc.		p.
2.	Lands, fem.	gen.			p.
3.	Prophets, masc.	acc.			p.
4.	Tongues, fem.	dat.	abl.		p.
5.	Churches, fem.	dat.	abl.		p.
6.	Scriptures, fem.	acc.			p.
7.	Souls, fem. nom.	voc.			p.
8.	Thanks, fem.	acc.			p.
9.	Languages, fem.	dat.	abl.		p.
10.	Souls, fem.	gen.			p.

Exercise 5

1. We shall praise you without end. 1st.

2. The Saviour of the world will reign over us. 1st.

3. All flesh will see the salvation of our God. 2nd.

4. I shall adore at your holy temple. 1st.

5. I shall call on the name of the Lord. 1st.

6. Blessed are the pure in heart, for they will see God. 2nd.

7. Blessed are the meek, for they will possess the earth. 2nd.

8. The Lord will reveal the things hidden. 1st.

9. I shall sing to the Lord, who has done good things to me. 1st.

10. In the evil day the Lord will set free the poor man. 1st.

Exercise 6

1. All the earth will say a psalm to your name, O most high. 3rd.

2. In his temple all will tell of his glory. 3rd.

3. I shall live, and shall tell of the works of the Lord. 1st.

4. I shall seek your face, O Lord. 3rd.

5. I shall not leave you orphans: I shall come to you again, alleluia. 3rd, 4th.

6. This Jesus, who has been taken up from you into heaven, in the same way will come again. 4th.

7. They will cast out devils: they will lay their hands on the sick and they will be cured (literally: they will have well). 5th, 3rd, 2nd.

8. In the day of my resurrection I shall go before you into Galilee. 3rd.

9. Who will go up into the mountain of the Lord, or who will stand in his holy place? 3rd, 1st.

10. This man will take (receive) a blessing from the Lord. 5th.

Exercise 7

1. Lamb, m. nom. voc. s. God, m. gen. s.
   Lamb of God, who takes away the sins of the world, have mercy on us.

2. Lord, m. dat. abl. s. God. m. dat. s. Let us give thanks *to the Lord* our God.

3. Lord. m. acc. s. God, m. acc. s. To pray for me *to the Lord* our God.

4. God, m. acc. s. God, m. abl. s. True *God* from true *God.*

5. Servant, m. acc. s. Lord, m. voc. s. Now you let your *servant* depart, O *Lord.*

6. Lord, m. nom. s. Place, m. abl. s. The *Lord* is in his holy *place.*

7. Lord, m. acc. s. Christ, m. acc. s. Son, m. acc. s. Through our *Lord* Jesus *Christ* your *Son.*

8. Angel, m. gen. s. By the hands of your holy *angel.*

9. Angel, m. nom, s. Lord, m. gen. s. The *Angel* of the *Lord* declared unto Mary.

10. Lord, m. voc. s. God, m. nom. voc. s. *Lord God,* heavenly king.

Exercise 8

1. Apostles, m. nom. p.
   The blessed apostles Peter and Paul.

2. Servants, m. dat. p.
   Deign to grant to us also, your sinful servants.

3. Heavens, m. nom. p. Earth, f. nom, s.
   Glory, f. abl. s. The heavens and the earth are full of your glory.

4. Hymns, m. abl. p.
   Sion, praise your Saviour in hymns and canticles.

5. Christ, m. gen. s. Hell, m. acc. p. We recall the descent of Christ to Hell.

6. Lord, m. voc. s. Eyes, m. acc. p. I have lifted up my eyes to you, O Lord.

7. Servants, m. nom. p. Lord, m. voc. s. And so we your servants are mindful, O Lord.

8. Disciples, m. dat. p.
   He blessed and gave (it) to his disciples.

9. Apostles, m. abl. p.
   With your holy Apostles and Martyrs.

10. Angels, m. nom. p. Heavens, m. nom. p. gen. p.
    The angels praise your majesty, the Dominations adore (you), and the heights of the heavens rejoice together.

Exercise 9

1. The men fear the Lord.

2. The Lord's disciples will sing a hymn.

3. The Lord loves the boy.

4. The angels adore the Lord.

5. The eyes of the apostles look upon the Lord.

6. The archangels praise the Son of God.

7. The disciples fear hell.

8. The prophets hope for mercy.

9. The Lord's servants will hear a hymn.

10. God strengthens the church by grace.

Exercise 10

1. The servants of the Lord carry gifts.
2. The Lord accepts the sacrifice.
3. For ever and ever (literally: 'into ages of ages').
4. The apostle proclaims the gospel.
5. The word of the Lord: thanks be to God.
6. May your kingdom come.
7. Mary says: They have no wine.
8. My help is from the Lord.
9. Lamb of God, who takes away the sins of the world …
10. Let us adore eternally the most holy sacrament.

Exercise 11

1. The Lord always loves (his) servant.
2. Today the angels adore God.
3. The king was praying confidently.
4. The Church proclaims the gospel here and everywhere.
5. Lord, now you let your servant depart.
6. We happily receive the word of God.
7. The Lord faithfully guards the Church.
8. Lord, I have sinned very much.
9. Lord, only say the word and my soul will be healed.
10. The Lord rose again wonderfully: now truly he lives.

Exercise 12

1. The children were carrying branches in their hands.
2. They were crying out in a loud voice, saying: Hosanna in excelsis.
3. The children of the Hebrews spread out their garments on the road, saying: Hosanna to the son of David.
4. Jesus said: I kept safe those whom you gave me.
5. Many suffering from diseases kept coming to him, and he healed them all.
6. I kept God always in my sight.
7. It was necessary for Christ to suffer and to rise again from the dead on the third day.
8. When you were a young man, you girded yourself, and walked where you wished.
9. The old man was carrying the boy; but the boy ruled the old man.
10. That fire appeared above the disciples.

Exercise 13

1. You alone (are) holy.
2. I shall proclaim your holy gospel.
3. I believe in one Lord Jesus Christ.
4. The only-begotten Son of God.
5. True God from true God.
6. And in the Holy Spirit.
7. And in one holy, catholic and apostolic Church.
8. Blessed (be) God for ever.
9. It is fitting and right to give thanks to the Lord our God.
10. Lord, I am not worthy.

Exercise 14

1. Lord, I am not worthy.
2. Blessed are you, Lord God of all creation.

3. This is my body …this is the cup …
4. The heavens and the earth are full of (filled with) your glory.
5. Blessed be the God and Father of our Lord Jesus Christ.
6. You alone are holy, you alone are Lord.
7. The mystery of faith.
8. Truly, Lord, you are holy.
9. Our Father, who art in heaven.
10. With prayer and hymns, we stand before you.

Exercise 15

1. He was in the world, and the world did not recognise him.
2. You will not be servants, but friends.
3. The apostles were disciples of the Lord.
4. We were servants of the Lord.
5. Christ will be Lord for ever.
6. The saints will always be blessed.
7. O God, you will always be just and great.
8. The holy scriptures were in the churches.
9. We are the friends of Christ.
10. Christ was, is (and) will be Lord.

Exercise 16

1. We offer these gifts for your holy Church, together with our Pope N.
2. You accepted the sacrifice of Abraham our patriarch.
3. Lord, you accept these gifts on the feast of blessed John the Baptist.
4. Who spoke through the holy prophets.
5. Lord, we praise your glory (shown) in the prophet blessed John the Baptist.

Exercise 17

1. This is the cup of my blood.
2. This is my body.
3. In the name of the Father and of the Son and of the Holy Spirit. Amen.
4. I have sinned very much, in thought, word, deed and omission.
5. Therefore I beseech blessed Mary ever Virgin … and you brothers, to pray for me …
6. Glory to God in the highest, and on earth peace to men of good will.
7. I believe in one God, the Father almighty, maker of heaven and of earth.
8. God from God, light from light.
9. I acknowledge one baptism for (into) the forgiveness of sins.
10. Lord, we proclaim your death and acknowledge your resurrection.

Exercise 17a

Pater, nomen, volúntas, panem, debitóribus, tentatiónem.

Exercise 18

1. Those who trust in the Lord are like mount Sion.
2. Come, O Holy Spirit, and kindle in them the fire of your love.
3. Come, O light of (our) hearts.
4. Send out your light and your truth: which lead me into your holy mountain.
5. The Spirit of the Lord has filled the earth (literally: the globe of lands).
6. Enlighten our hearts with the splendour of your grace.
7. Wash me … and I shall be made whiter than snow.

8. Joining together and celebrating the most holy night …
9. Christ visibly appeared in the reality of our flesh.
10. Come, O Holy Spirit … visit the minds of your people.

Exercise 19

1. He took bread into his holy and venerable hands.
2. Who, on account of us men and for our salvation came down from heaven (the heavens).
3. And he rose again on the third day, according to the scriptures.
4. And he ascended into heaven, (and) sits at the right hand of the Father.
5. Pray, brothers, that my sacrifice and yours may become acceptable in the presence of God.
6. Lord, (you) who sit above the Cherubim, stir up your power and come.
7. Through our Lord Jesus Christ. Amen.
8. And (he was) born of the Father before all ages.
9. You have freed us through your cross and resurrection.
10. I have lifted up my soul to you, O Lord.

Exercise 20

1. Glory to God in the highest, and on earth peace to men.
2. And (he was) born of the Father before all ages.
3. God from God, light from light, true God from true God.
4. (He was) also crucified for us.
5. Who with the Father and the Son is at the same time adored and glorified.
6. We give you thanks because you have considered us worthy to stand in your presence.
7. We sing a hymn to your glory, saying without end, Holy …
8. Through him, and with him, and in him, is to you, Father … all honour and glory.
9. From the rising of the sun to the setting, a pure oblation may be offered to your name.
10. For he himself, on that night that he was betrayed, took bread.

Exercise 21

1. Christ rising again from the dead has renewed life.
2. Christ visibly appeared in the reality of our flesh.
3. Through your death you have given life to the world.
4. The Holy Spirit filled the womb of blessed Mary by his power.
5. O Lord, to you I have lifted up my soul.
6. Through the Virgin Mary we have been worthy to receive your Son, the author of life.
7. Lord, look on the victim which you yourself have prepared for your Church.
8. Christ, in his first coming in the lowliness of flesh, fulfilled the purpose of the ancient order.
9. Christ proclaimed the good news of salvation to the poor, to prisoners freedom, and to those in sorrow, joy.
10. The heavens are yours and the earth is yours; you founded the whole earth (literally: globe of lands).

Exercise 22a

> fecísti — you have made
> condidísti — you have established
> commisísti — you have entrusted
> (non) dereliquísti — you have (not) abandoned
> subvenísti — you have assisted
> obtulísti — you have offered
> erudísti — you have instructed

Exercise 22b

1. I saw water coming out of the temple … and all those whom that water reached were saved.
2. Blessed are you, O God, because from your bounty we have received bread.

3. Be mindful also of our brothers, who have fallen asleep in the hope of the resurrection.

4. The Virgin Mary conceived your only-begotten Son by the overshadowing of the Holy Spirit.

5. Blessed are you, who have come in the abundance of your mercy.

6. He took bread into his holy and venerable hands.

7. He has made the peoples subject to us, and (placed) the nations under our feet.

8. And my spirit has rejoiced in God my salvation, because he has looked on the lowliness of his handmaid.

9. The Hebrew people came with palms to meet you.

10. The Lord made clay out of spittle, and anointed my eyes, and I went away and washed, and I believed in God.

Exercise 23

1. Christ was sent to heal the contrite of heart.

2. It is truly fitting and just, and right for (our) salvation, for us always and everywhere to give thanks to you.

3. Cleanse my heart and my lips, so that I may be able worthily to proclaim your holy gospel.

4. Deign to keep in peace, preserve, keep in unity and rule your Church over the whole earth.

5. Rescue us from eternal damnation and command us to be numbered in the flock of your elect.

6. We have seen his star in the east, and have came with gifts to adore the Lord.

7. Make me always stay close to your commandments, and never allow me to be separated from you.

8. Therefore we offer this sacrifice to you for these (people), to whom you have deigned to give new life by (out of) water and the Holy Spirit.

9. You do not cease to gather a people to yourself.

10. Command that these gifts be carried by the hands of your holy Angel to your altar on high.

Exercise 24: see vocabulary for answers.

Exercise 24a

1. (You) who were sent to heal the contrite of heart, have mercy on us.

2. The Lamb has redeemed the sheep: the innocent Christ has reconciled sinners to the Father.

3. He gave thanks, and gave (it) to his disciples, saying: Take and drink of this, all (of you) …

4. He took the bread, and giving thanks he broke (it) and gave (it) to his disciples, saying …

5. We beseech you, O Lord, that these gifts may become the body and blood of Christ which he himself left us as an everlasting covenant.

Exercise 25

1. In the name of the Father, and of the Son, and of the Holy Spirit. Amen.

2. Glory be to the Father, and to the Son, and to the Holy Spirit.

3. The Lord be with you: and with your spirit.

4. The grace of our Lord Jesus Christ and the love of God, and the fellowship of the Holy Spirit be with you all.

5. Our Lord Jesus took bread …

6. Deign to look with a favourable and serene face upon these offerings.

7. Command that these offerings be carried into the sight of your divine majesty.

8. In (at) the name of the Lord let every knee be bent, of creatures in heaven, on earth, and below.

9. One thing I have sought from the Lord, this will I ask, that I may live in the house of the Lord.

10. So that from the rising of the sun until the setting a pure oblation may be offered to you.

Exercise 26

1. Rising from the dead, he gave us eternal life.

2. We give you thanks … Lord God, heavenly King, God the Father almighty.

3. In the same way, after supper had been eaten, taking also this most excellent cup …

4. Pray, brothers, that my sacrifice and yours may become acceptable.

5. I believe in the Father almighty, maker of heaven and earth, and of all things, visible and invisible.

6. The day before he suffered, he took bread into his holy and venerable hands.

7. The angels and archangels proclaim, saying with unceasing voice, 'Holy' …

8.   Be mindful, Lord, of all those standing around (your altar).

9.   Joining together and venerating the memory, in the first place of the glorious Virgin Mary …

10.   Through Jesus Christ your Son, we as supplicants ask and beseech …

Exercise 27

1.   And he rose again on the third day.

2.   Graciously give peace in our days.

3.   Remember also, O Lord, your servants and handmaids N. and N. who have gone before us with the sign of faith.

4.   Do not look on our sins, but on the faith of your Church.

5.   Looking forward to the blessed hope and coming of our Saviour Jesus Christ …

6.   Christ my hope is risen.

7.   O wonderful thing! A poor man, a servant and a wretch eat (the body of) the Lord.

8.   Under different appearances

   Only in signs and not in realities

   Precious things lie hidden.

9.   Together with your servant, our Pope N., and all true believers and those who practise the faith.

10.   And may you order our days in your peace.

Exercise 28

1.   Who with the Father and the Son at the same time is adored.

2.   We who are refreshed by the body and blood of your Son.

3.   For he himself, on the night that he was betrayed, took bread.

4.   Sprinkle me with hyssop, O Lord, and I shall be cleansed.

5.   Wash me and I shall be made whiter than snow.

6.   For this is my body, which will be given up for you.

7.   For this is the cup of my blood, which will be shed for you and for many.

8.   But only say the word and my soul shall be healed.

9.   All the people who await you, O Lord, will not be put to shame.

10.   Drop down dew, O heavens, from above, and the clouds will rain down the just one; the earth will be opened and will bring forth the Saviour.

Exercise 29

1.   All those to whom that water reached were saved.

2.   Through whom all things were made.

3.   And he was incarnate by the Holy Spirit of the Virgin Mary, and was made man.

4.   He was also crucified for us under Pontius Pilate, suffered and was buried.

5.   He was incarnate by the Holy Spirit, was changed into the form of our nature.

6.   By the word of God the heavens were established.

7.   Christ appeared to all the disciples, and was taken up into heaven.

8.   I rejoiced at (in) the things which were said to me.

9.   Listen favourably to your people, O God, upon whom your name is invoked.

10.   After his resurrection Christ was plainly seen by the disciples.

Exercise 30

1.   The Lord be with you

2.   We praise you, we bless you, we adore you, we glorify you.

3.   We give you thanks on account of your great glory.

4.   You alone (are) holy, you alone (are) the Lord, you alone (are) Most High.

5.   May the body of Christ preserve me to eternal life.

6.   Lamb of God, who takes away the sins of the world, have mercy on us.

7.   I am the bread of life.

8.   You have made known your ways to me.

9. O Saviour of the world, save us.

10. Therefore I beseech blessed Mary ever a Virgin, all the angels and saints, and you, brothers ...

Exercise 31

1. I have sinned very much, in thought, word, deed and omission, through my fault, through my fault, through my very great fault.

2. We give you thanks on account of your great glory.

3. The Lord heard their supplication.

4. May the Lord be in your heart and on your lips, so that you may worthily and ably proclaim his holy Gospel.

5. May the Lord accept the sacrifice from your hands, to the praise and glory of his name, and to our good and that of all his holy Church.

6. Through the mystery of this water and wine, may we be made partakers of his divinity, who deigned to become a sharer in our humanity.

7. Be mindful, O Lord, of your servants N. and N.; their faith is known to you, and their devotion known.

8. For this is the Cup of my Blood ... Do this in memory of me.

9. Do not look on our sins, but on the faith of your Church.

10. We proclaim your death, O Lord, and acknowledge your resurrection, until you come.

Exercise 32

1. I believe in one God ... And in one holy, catholic and apostolic Church.

2. Where two or three are gathered together in my name, I am there in the midst of them.

3. But now there remain these three, faith, hope, charity.

4. And in our one Lord.

5. Five virgins were foolish and five wise.

6. A thousand years before your eyes are like one day.

7. After eight days, the doors being closed, Jesus stood in their midst and said: Peace be with you.

8. I have chosen you twelve, and one (out) of you is a devil.

9. And he rose again on the third day.

10. Because you have wished to gather sons together in one, through the blood of your Son.

Exercise 33

1. I confess to almighty God ... that I have sinned very much.

2. Christ died and rose again for us.

3. Lamb of God, who takes away the sins of the world, have mercy on us.

4. He was also crucified for us, suffered and was buried.

5. And in the Holy Spirit ... who spoke through the prophets.

6. We acknowledge, Holy Father, that you are great.

7. From your bounty we receive bread ... from which will be made for us the bread of life.

8. Christ deigned to become a partaker of our humanity.

9. For these, O Lord, and for all who rest in Christ, we ask a place of refreshment, light and peace.

10. Through Christ our Lord, through whom you give all good things to the world.

Exercise 34

1. For this is my body.

2. Take, drink of this, all (of you); for this is the cup of my blood.

3. By the mystery of this water and wine may we be made partakers of his divinity.

4. Accept and bless these gifts, these offerings, these holy, unspotted sacrifices.

5. Joining together and celebrating the most holy night in which blessed Mary brought forth the Saviour to this world.

6. We therefore ask of you, O Lord, that you will be pleased to accept this offering of our service.

7. All those to whom that water reached were saved.

8. God himself is the Lord; he himself made us, and not we ourselves.

9. Through him and with him and in him is to you ... all honour and glory.

10. Be mindful also of those ...

Exercise 35

1. Through Christ our Lord, who lives and reigns for ever.
2. We have received bread, which we offer to you ... from which will be made for us the bread of life.
3. We have received wine, which we offer to you . .
4. Bless these gifts ... which we offer to you.
5. The Lord looks on all the people standing around (the altar) ... whose faith in him is known and devotion recognised, (and) for whom we offer ...
6. Joining together and celebrating the most holy night in which blessed Mary brought forth the Saviour to this world.
7. For this is my body which will be given up for you.
8. For this is the cup of my blood ... which will be shed for you and for many.
9. Our Father, who art in heaven.
10. Blessed are they who are called to the supper of the Lamb.

Exercise 36

1. From your bounty we have received bread, which we offer to you.
2. To you they offer the sacrifice of praise, for themselves and for all their (people).
3. The sacrifice which your high priest Melchisedech offered to you.
4. Command that these things be carried by the hand of your holy Angel to your altar on high.
5. Deign to make holy, O Lord, these gifts, which we bring to you to be sanctified.
6. Look upon ... the victim ... by whose sacrifice you wished to be appeased.
7. But many times you also offered covenants to man.
8. Be mindful also of those who have died in the peace of your Christ.
9. I rejoiced at those things which were said to me.
10. The gifts of your Church, in which now are set forth not gold, frankincense and myrrh, but Jesus Christ.

Exercise 37

1. Who is this King of glory?
2. Tell us, Mary, what did you see on (your) way?
3. The Lord is my light and my salvation: whom shall I fear?
4. The Lord is the defender of my life, of whom shall I be afraid?
5. Where is their God?
6. Why, O Lord, do you grow angry with your people?
7. Who shall go up into the mountain of the Lord?
8. O God, my God, look on me: why have you abandoned me?
9. You men of Galilee, why do you wonder, looking up into heaven?
10. If you, O Lord, shall take notice of our evil deeds, Lord who will endure?

Exercise 38

1. It is not lawful to put anyone to death.
2. A hymn is fitting — ('to be sung' understood) — for you O God in Sion

Exercise 39

1. Lamb of God, who takes away the sins of the world, give us peace.
2. Look, we beseech you, at the offering of your Church.
3. Take and eat of this, all (of you): for this is my body.
4. (You) who take away the sins of the world ... receive our prayer.
5. O Saviour of the world, save us.
6. Give us this day our daily bread.
7. Forgive us our trespasses.

8. But deliver us from evil.

9. Sanctify, we beg you, O Lord, these offerings of our service …

10. Offer to you (= to each other) peace (a sign of peace).

Exercise 39a

Veni	Reple	Fove
Emítte	Lava	Rege
Veni	Riga	Da
Veni	Sana	Da
Veni	Flecte	Da
		Da

Exercise 40

1. Have mercy on us, O Lord.

2. Turn, O Lord, and rescue my soul.

3. Be pleased, O Lord, we pray you, with the prayers of our humility.

4. Seek the Lord, and be strengthened: always seek his face.

5. Say to the faint-hearted: Be comforted.

6. Jesus, have mercy on us: feed us, protect us.

7. O God, be merciful to your departed servants.

8. Therefore now, O Lord, be mindful of all the people for whom we offer this sacrifice to you.

9. Acknowledge the Lord, for he is good.

10. Lift up your heads, O gates, and be lifted up, you everlasting doors.

Exercise 41

1. You alone are the Lord, you alone are most high, Jesus Christ.

2. The Lord says to Peter: When you were younger, you girded yourself …

3. Joining together and celebrating the most holy day of the resurrection of our Lord Jesus Christ …

4. Deliver us, O Lord, from all evils, and mercifully give peace in our days …

5. The judgements of the Lord are right, and sweeter than honey and the honeycomb.

6. O Lord, we most faithfully implore your mercy.

7. O bountiful Mother of the Redeemer, Virgin before and after (giving birth).

8. O God, who wonderfully established the dignity of human nature, and still more wonderfully renewed it …

9. Therefore, O most merciful Father, we humbly ask and beg you …

10. O God, may you deign by your word to feed us more inwardly.

Exercise 42

1. O Lord, hasten to help me.

2. (You) who sit at the right hand of the Father, to intercede for us: Lord have mercy.

3. To see me is to see the Father.

4. O God, you show your all-powerfulness in sparing (us) and having mercy (on us).

5. By being born Christ bestowed on us many joys.

6. In dying he destroyed our death, and in rising again restored our life.

7. A nature bound unavoidably to die saddens us, but the promise of immortality comforts us.

8. The tribes of the Lord went up to Jerusalem, to acknowledge your name, O Lord.

9. Christ went around doing good and healing all those afflicted by the devil.

10. May your family come to Christ, by following the words of John the Forerunner.

Exercise 43

1. O Lord, we hasten with gifts to venerate (your) altars.

2. O God, you have beneficially established a time to restore the purity of our minds.

3. You have come together in order to celebrate the feast of the Virgin Mary.

4. By a wonderful fellowship, he has brought us also back to everlasting (life).

5. May the receiving of your body, O Lord, be of benefit to me as a healing remedy.
6. Grant, O Lord, to your people to come to the incorruptible resurrection of (their) flesh which is to be glorified.
7. Death and life fought together in a amazing conflict.
8. Grant to us, O Lord, that we may come to understand the hidden mystery of Christ.
9. That which Christ did at the supper, he said must be done in his memory.
10. Paul was the master and teacher of the nations (that) were to be called.

Exercise 44

1. Be mindful of your servant N. whom you have today called from the world.
2. Make us, we beseech you, O Lord, to be filled with the everlasting enjoyment of your divinity.
3. Go, the Mass is ended.
4. Lord, I am not worthy that you should enter under my roof, but only say the word and my soul shall be healed.
5. Make me always remain firm to your commandments.
6. O Lord, be merciful to our sins.
7. Say to us, Mary, what did you see on (your) way?
8. Be mindful also of our brothers, who have fallen asleep in the hope of the resurrection.
9. Mercifully be attentive to our petitions, O Lord.
10. Make us, we beseech you, O Lord, profit from the frequenting of heavenly things.

Exercise 45

1. The judgements of the Lord are right, making glad the hearts (of men).
2. O God, the protector of those who hope in you, without whom nothing is sound, nothing holy …
3. The Lord is close to all those calling upon him.
4. Grant to us that, keeping your ordinances, we may be worthy to attain to perpetual life.
5. Joining together, and celebrating the most holy day … and venerating the memory (of) …
6. Taking also this excellent cup into his holy and venerable hands …
7. There was a man named Job, simple and upright and fearing God.
8. They sing together a hymn to your glory, saying ceaselessly: Holy, holy, holy …
9. Teach all nations, baptising them in the name of the Father, and of the Son, and of the Holy Spirit.
10. I saw the tomb of the living Christ and the glory of the risen one.

Exercise 46

only-begotten, born, begotten, made, made
incarnate, crucified, suffered, buried, about to come
spoken, about to come

Exercise 47

1. He took bread, and having lifted up (his) eyes to heaven, he gave (it) to his disciples.
2. O Lord Jesus Christ, in working together with the Holy Spirit, you gave life to the world through your death.
3. Grant to your faithful people, their minds having been made pure, to be led to the fullness of the sons of grace.
4. O God, you anointed your only-begotten Son, all creatures having been made subject to his rule, with the oil of rejoicing.
5. Make us, O Lord, our minds having been freed from disordered inclinations, adhere to things eternal.
6. After eight days, the doors being closed, Jesus stood in the midst of his disciples and said: Peace be with you.
7. May almighty God have mercy on us, and, our sins having been forgiven, may he lead us to eternal life.
8. The pledge of eternal redemption being received, we celebrate the mystery of the nativity.
9. John the Baptist, by the shedding of his blood, was worthy to show the highest witness to Christ.
10. O God, our inner vision made clear, may we rejoice to see your glory.

Exercise 48

1. Come, Lord Jesus, and do not delay.
2. Bless the Lord, O my soul, and do not forget all his rewards.
3. Put in your hand and feel the places of the nails, and do not be unbelieving.

4. Neither do I condemn you: now sin no more.

5. Be comforted, you faint-hearted, and do not be afraid.

Exercise 49

1. Brothers, let us acknowledge our sins.

2. May the Lord accept the sacrifice from your hands, to the praise and glory of his name.

3. The peace of the Lord be always with you.

4. Let us give thanks to the Lord our God.

5. The grace of our Lord Jesus Christ, and the love of God, … be with you all.

6. (May) thy will be done, on earth as (it is) in heaven.

7. Never let me be separated from you.

8. May the Lord be in your heart and on your lips.

9. May the body of Christ keep me to eternal life.

10. May almighty God bless you, the Father, the Son and the Holy Spirit.

Exercise 50

1. In you, O Lord I have hoped: may I not be confounded.

2. By the gospel words may our sins be blotted out.

3. Deign to keep in peace, guard, keep in unity and rule your Church, over the whole world.

4. By the mystery of this water and wine may we become partakers in his divinity.

5. Hallowed be thy name; thy kingdom come.

6. In a spirit of humility and with a contrite heart, may we be received by you, O Lord.

7. May we be filled with all heavenly grace and blessing.

8. May we be found one body and one spirit in Christ.

9. O Lord, let me not be put to confusion, for I have called upon you.

10. Through his passion and cross may we be led to the glory of the resurrection.

Exercise 51

1. Do not look upon our sins, but on the faith of your Church.

2. And lead us not into temptation.

3. Do not forget the souls of your poor at the last.

4. Deliver them from the mouth of the lion, may hell not swallow them up, (and) let them not fall into darkness.

5. Do not turn your face away from me.

Exercise 52

1. We therefore pray, O Lord, that you be pleased to accept this offering of our service.

2. We humbly ask and beg that you accept and bless these gifts.

3. Grant, we pray, that we may experience the intercession of blessed Mary (literally : blessed Mary to intercede for us).

4. Pray, brothers, that my sacrifice and yours may be acceptable in the presence of God the almighty Father.

5. Therefore I beseech blessed Mary ever a virgin, all the angels and saints, and you, brothers, to pray for me to the Lord our God.

6. We beseech that you grant to these, O Lord, and to all who rest in Christ, a place of refreshment, light and peace.

7. Make us, almighty God, to exult in holy joys, and to rejoice in the holy giving of thanks for the ascension of your Son.

8. Grant that you nourish in us those things which are good, and preserve those things which have come to fulfilment (literally: which are nourished) .

9. Grant that in the sharing of the mystery you may teach us to cling to heavenly things.

10. One thing I have asked from the Lord, this I will seek, that I may dwell in the house of the Lord.

Exercise 52a

concede

da

tribue

praesta

Exercise 53

1. May our sacrifice in your sight today be made in such a way as may be pleasing to you.
2. As much as you can, dare so much,
   For (he is) above all praise,
   Neither can you praise enough.
3. Thy will be done on earth as (it is) in heaven.
4. Grant to your servants that they may for ever contemplate you, (their) maker and redeemer.
5. Sanctify, therefore, these gifts, we pray you, that they may become for us the body and blood of your most beloved Son.
6. We beseech you that they may be able happily to attain eternal life.
7. May this mingling of the Body and Blood of our Lord Jesus Christ bring eternal life to us receiving it.
8. Grant, O Lord, that we may be able to come to you, pure in heart.
9. May the gifts which we offer become for us the price of your eternal redemption.
10. Grant to us, O Lord, to be partakers in his divinity, who deigned to be made a sharer in our humanity.

Exercise 54

1. The Lord be in your heart and on your lips, so that you may worthily and competently proclaim his Gospel.
2. Remember, O Lord, your Church, that you may perfect it in love.
3. May God make his face to shine over us, that we may known his way on earth.
4. And in (their) hands they will bear you, lest you strike your foot against a stone.
5. The Son of man came that he might give his soul for the redemption of many.
6. O God, you anointed your Son with the oil of rejoicing, so that he might deliver the kingdom to your great majesty.
7. You have come to the aid of all people, so that those seeking you should find (you).
8. The Lord gave himself up to death, so that he might destroy death and renew life.
9. May our prayers ascend to you, O Lord, so that we may be fitted for your sacraments.
10. I will give you another Advocate that he might remain with you for ever.

Exercise 55

1. Blessed are you, O Lord, God of all things, because from your bounty we have received bread.
2. We offer you (this) cup, giving thanks because you have held us worthy to stand in your presence and serve you .
3. Truly you are holy, O Lord, because through your Son, with the working of the strength of the Holy Spirit, you give life to, and sanctify, all things.
4. We give thanks to you, because you alone (are) holy, you alone (are) the Lord, you alone (are) most high, O Jesus Christ.
5. Truly it is right and just to give you thanks, because today you have revealed in Christ the mystery of our salvation .
6. We acknowledge you, O holy Father, because you are great and have made all your works in wisdom and love.
7. Let the heavens rejoice and let the earth exult before the face of the Lord, for he will come.
8. Come, you people, and adore the Lord: because today a great light has come down on the earth.
9. And the king will desire your beauty because he is your lord, and (you) honour him.
10. You are indeed happy, O holy Virgin Mary, and most worthy of all praise: because out of you is risen the sun of justice, Christ our God.

Exercise 56

1. In the same way, after supper had been eaten, taking also this excellent cup … he blessed (it).
2. The Lord said to Peter: When you were younger, you girded yourself and walked where you wished.
3. As often as we eat this bread and drink (from) this cup, we proclaim your death, O Lord, until you come.
4. When the chief steward had tasted the water made into wine, he said to the bridegroom …
5. While all things kept silence, midway through the night, your almighty word came down from heaven, from the royal throne (literally: thrones).
6. We proclaim your death, O Lord, and acknowledge your resurrection, until you come.
7. Before I formed you in the womb I knew you: and before you came out of the womb I sanctified you.
8. Grant that he who has died in Christ may live in him, when he will raise up the dead in (their) flesh from the earth.
9. Who, when he was given up willingly to his passion, took bread and, giving thanks, broke (it).
10. Before Philip had called you, when you were under the fig tree, I saw you.

Exercise 57

1. Therefore when the Holy Spirit comes, he will proclaim all things to us.

2. When he comes a second time in the glory of his majesty, we will openly receive (our) reward.

3. If anyone hears (will have heard) my word and does not keep it (will not have kept it), I do not judge him.

4. From whatever trouble they cry (will have cried) to me, I will hear them.

5. Blessed is the servant who, when the Lord comes (will have come) he finds (will have found) watching .

6. Wherever the body is, to that place also will the eagles be gathered together.

7. When Christ appears, we shall be like him, for we shall see him as he is.

8. But when you grow old, you will stretch out your hands, and another will gird you, and lead you where you do not wish.

9. The bread which I will give is my flesh for the life of the world.

10. When I shall have ascended to my Father, I will send the Comforter to you.

Exercise 58

1. Graciously give peace in our days.

2. He came down from heaven … and he ascended into heaven, (and) sits at the right hand of the Father.

3. From the rising of the sun to the setting may a pure sacrifice be offered to your name.

4. Glory to God in the highest, and on earth peace to men of good will.

5. Truly it is fitting and right … to acknowledge you, and especially in this day more gloriously to proclaim (you), when Christ our Passover was sacrificed for us.

6. After eight days, the doors being closed, Jesus stood in the midst of the disciples.

7. May the body of Christ preserve me to eternal life.

8. And therefore remembering, O Lord the so blessed passion, and not only the resurrection from the dead, but also the glorious ascension into heaven, of your Son Jesus Christ …

9. And in Jesus Christ … born of the Father before all ages.

10. O God, my God, from the light (i.e. daybreak) I watch for you.

Exercise 59

1. May Peter lead us by the key, Paul by the word, to our native land, to which they deserved happily to pass, one by the cross, the other by the sword.

2. May the humility of the flock attain to that place whence came forth the endurance of the shepherd.

3. You provide for us a remedy for that mortality, and whoever was lost, from whatever cause they had perished, from that you saved them.

4. The man who at his birth had brought many joys was he who, alone of all the prophets, showed openly the lamb of redemption.

5. (We) his members trust that we will follow to that place where he, our head, has gone before.

Exercise 60

1. So be converted that your sins may be blotted out.

2. He was led as the sheep to the slaughter, so that he did not open his mouth.

3. May we so make use of joys that pass away as to enable us presently to dwell among the joys that will endure.

4. O God, you so loved the world that you sent us the Saviour.

5. May our sacrifice be such in your sight today as to be pleasing to you.

Exercise 61

1. Forgive us our trespasses as we forgive those who trespass against us.

2. Deign to look upon (this) bread and cup, as you consented to accept the offering of your just servant Abel.

3. The just man will flourish like the palm tree: like the cedar which is in Lebanon he shall be increased.

4. May he grant that as Christ was seen after his resurrection, so may he be pleased to appear before you for all eternity.

5. As much as you can, that much dare,

   For (he is) greater than all praise,

   Neither do you do enough to praise.

6. One eats (of it), a thousand eat,

   As much they, so much he,

   Neither is what is eaten consumed.

7. Thy will be done on carth, as it is in hcavcn.

8. They who trust in the Lord (are) like Mount Sion: he will not be moved for ever who dwells in Jerusalem.

9. As much as we are full of dread because of what we deserve, so much do we trust in your kindness.

10. May we proceed in deeper devotion, the nearer the day that brings salvation approaches.

Exercise 62

1. (He) who believes in me, (even) if he has died, he will live.

2. If you love me, keep my commandments, says the Lord.

3. If you wish, you can make me clean.

4. If anyone hears my voice, and opens the door to me, I will come in to him.

5. Unless the grain of corn, falling to the ground, dies, it will remain itself alone.

6. But if it dies, it will bear much fruit.

7. Father, if this cup cannot pass from me unless I drink it, your will be done.

8. If he were not a criminal, we would not have given him up to you.

9. Who can forgive sins, except God alone?

10. If anyone eats of this bread, he will live for ever.

Exercise 63

1. We know that Christ has truly risen from the dead.

2. I confess to almighty God, that I have sinned very much.

3. You have thought us worthy to stand in your presence.

4. O Lord, I have believed that you are the Christ, the Son of the living God, who came into this world.

5. Did you not know that it is my duty to be about these matters which concern my Father?

6. John the Baptist prophesied that Christ would come, and showed that he was present.

7. Today you will know that the Lord will come and save us.

8. We acknowledge Christ your servant was sent to preach the gospel to the poor.

9. Simeon received an answer from the Holy Spirit that he should not die until he had seen Christ the Lord.

10. We believe through a voice from heaven that your Word lives among men.

Exercise 64

1. Therefore I beseech blessed Mary ever a virgin.

2. Christ is baptised by John in the Jordan.

3. He was crucified also for us under Pontius Pilate.

4. The Lord said to the Samaritan woman: Give me to drink (= something to drink).

5. By the sea of Galilee the Lord saw the two brothers Peter and Andrew, and he called them.

6. And he was incarnate by the Holy Spirit of the Virgin Mary.

7. Simon, son of John, do you love me?

8. The Lord saw the sisters of Lazarus weeping at the tomb; he cried: Lazarus, come out!

9. May the holy standard-bearer Michael lead them into the holy light.

10. Hail Mary, full of grace, the Lord is with thee.

Exercise 65

1. Lord Jesus Christ, Son of the living God, have mercy on us.

2. The Lord came into the city of Jerusalem.

3. Andrew said to Simon his brother: We have found the Messiah, who is called Christ; and he led him to Jesus.

4. You gave a promise to Abraham, and to his descendants for ever.

5. There were people on the road going up to Jerusalem.

6. Jesus said to his disciples: All power is given to me in heaven and on earth.

7. You deigned to accept the sacrifice of Abraham our Patriarch.

8. The Body and Blood of Jesus Christ.

9. Through Jesus Christ our Lord.

10. Jerusalem, Jerusalem, turn again to the Lord your God.

Exercise 66

1. Lord, you have turned away the captivity of Jacob.

2. Behold a virgin will conceive and will bear a son: and his name will be called Emmanuel.

3. Your high priest Melchisedech offered you a sacrifice.

4. Blessed be the Lord God of Israel.

5. The kings of Tarshish and the islands offer presents: the kings of the Arabians and of Seba bring gifts.

6. You who rule Israel, listen: you who lead Joseph like a sheep: you who sit above the Cherubim, appear in the presence of Ephraim, Benjamin and Manasses.

7. This is the generation of those who seek the face of the God of Jacob.

8. Sion, praise the Saviour.

9. The staff of Jesse has flowered.

10. There was a man in the land called Job: Satan asked God that he might tempt him.

VOCABULARY

Note to Readers

NOUNS are given with the nominative and genitive singular (from which you can tell the declension) and their gender: masculine, feminine or neuter (m. f. n.).

VERBS are given with their four principal parts (see lesson 24) and their conjugation. Some verbs lack one or more of their principal parts: this is shown by a dash. For '5th' conjugation see note in Lesson 22.

ADJECTIVES (adj.) are given with their singular m. f. and n. endings. From these it can clearly be seen whether they belong to group 1 or 2 (see lessons 13 and 26).

PRONOUNS (pron.) are also given with their m. f. and n. forms.

PREPOSITIONS (prep.) are shown with the case that normally follows them.

Other abbreviations:

adv.	— adverb	dep.	— deponent
conj.	— conjunction	num.	— numeral
impers.	— impersonal verb	irreg.	— irregular
indecl.	— indeclinable noun	interrog.	— interrogative
pl.	— plural	possess.	— possessive

A, AB (+ ablative), prep.	from
ABBA, (Aramaic — indecl.)	'Father'
ÁBEO, abíre, abívi (ábii), ábitum, irreg.	to go away
ABJÉCTIO, abjectiónis, f.	outcast, rejection, dejection
ÁBLUO, ablúere, áblui, ablútum, 3	to wash away
ABSÓLVO, absólvere, absólvi, absolútum, 3	to absolve
ABSÓRBEO, absorbére, absórbui, absórptum, 2	to swallow up, devour
ABSQUE (+ abl.), prep.	without, except, besides
ABSTÉRGEO, abstergére, abstérsi, abstérsum, 2	to wipe away, blot out
ABSTÍNEO, abstinére, abstínui, absténtum, 2	to refrain from, abstain
ABUNDÁNTER, adv.	abundantly
ABUNDÁNTIA, abundántiae, f.	abundance, prosperity
ABÚNDO, abundáre, abundávi, abundátum, 1	to overflow, be abundant
AC, conj.	and
ACCÉDO, accédere, accéssi, accéssum, 3	to come, approach
ACCÉNDO, accéndere, accéndi, accénsum, 3	to set on fire, inflame
ACCEPTÁBILIS, acceptábile, adj.	acceptable
ACCÉPTO, acceptáre, acceptávi, acceptátum, 1	to accept, receive with pleasure
ACCÍPIO, accípere, accépi, accéptum, 5	to receive, accept, take
ACCRÉSCO, accréscere, accrévi, accrétum, 3	to grow, increase
ACÉTUM, acéti, n.	vinegar
ACQUÍRO, acquírere, acquisívi, acquisítum, 3	to procure, obtain
ACQUISÍTIO, acquisitiónis, f.	purchase, acquisition
ÁCTIO, actiónis, f.	act, action
ACTUS, actus, m.	act, deed
AD (+ accusative), prep.	to, towards
ADDÚCO, addúcere, addúxi, addúctum, 3	to bring
ÁDEO, adíre, adívii, áditum, irreg.	to approach, come near to
ADEPS, ádipis, m. or f.	fat, marrow, the best or finest parts
ADHÍBEO, adhibére, adhíbui, adhíbitum, 2	to summon, invite
ADHUC, adv.	thus far, until now, still
ADÍMPLEO, adimplére, adimplévi, adimplétum, 2	to fill up
ADIPÍSCOR, adipísci, adéptus sum, 3 dep.	to come up to, reach, obtain
ÁDITUS, áditus, m.	approach, entrance
ADJÍCIO, adjícere, adjéci, adjéctum, 5	to add
ADJUMÉNTUM, adjuménti, n.	help, assistance
ADJÚNGO, adjúngere, adjúnxi, adjúnctum, 3	to join to
ADJUTÓRIUM adjutórii, n.	help, shelter, protection

ÁDJUVO, adjuváre, adjúvi, adjútum, 1	to help
ADMIRÁBILIS, admirábile, adj.	wonderful, admirable
ADMÍROR, admirári, admirátus sum, 1, dep.	to wonder at
ADMÍTTO, admíttere, admísi, admíssum, 3	to allow, admit
ADÓPTIO, adoptiónis, f.	adoption
ADÓRNO, adornáre, adornávi, adornátum, 1	to decorate, adorn
ADÓRO, adoráre, adorávi, adorátum, 1	to adore
ADSCRÍBO, adscríbere, adscrípsi, adscríptum, 3	to enrol, put on a list, approve
ADSUM, adésse, ádfui, irreg.	to be present, assist or defend
ÁDUMBRO, adumbráre, adumbrávi, adumbrátum, 1	to sketch out, give an idea of
ADÚNO, adunáre, adunávi, adunátum, 1	to unite
ADVÉNIO, adveníre, advéni, advéntum, 4	to come to, arrive at
ADVÉNTUS, advéntus, m.	a coming, arrival
ADVÉRSUS, advérsa, advérsum, adj.	hostile, unfavourable
ADVÉRSUS (+ acc.), prep.	against
ADVOCÁTIO, advocatiónis, f.	a pleading on another's behalf, advocacy
AEDIFICÁTIO, aedificatiónis, f.	1. a building of a house (action)
	2. a building, edifice
AEDÍFICO aedificáre, aedificávi, aedificátum, 1	to build
AEGER, aegra, aegrum, adj.	sick, ill
AEQUÁLITAS, aequalitátis, f.	equality
AÉQUITAS, aequitátis, f.	fairness, impartiality
AEQUUS, aequa, aequum, adj.	equal, right
AERÚMNA, aerúmnae, f.	hardship, affliction
AESTIMÁTOR, aestimatóris, m.	judge
ÁESTIMO, aestimáre, aestimávi, aestimátum, 1	to reckon, estimate (of moral worth)
AESTUS, aestus, m.	flaring heat; surge or tide
AETERNÁLIS, aeternále, adj.	eternal
AETÉRNITAS, aeternitátis, f.	eternity
AETÉRNUS, aetérna, aetérnum, adj.	eternal
	(IN AETÉRNUM: for ever)
AFFÉCTUS, afféctus, m.	devotion, love, desire, passion
ÁFFERO, áfferre, áttuli, allátum, irreg.	to bring up, bring forth, produce
AGNÓSCO, agnóscere, agnóvi, ágnitum, 3	to acknowledge
AGNUS, agni, m.	lamb (irreg. voc. sing. *agnus*)
AGO, ágere, egi, actum, 3	to do, act
	(GRÁTIAS ÁGERE — to give thanks)
ÁLACER (ÁLACRIS), álacre, adj.	quick, active, cheerful
ALÁCRITER, adv.	eagerly
ALIMÉNTUM, aliménti, n.	food, refreshment
ALIMÓNIUM, alimónii, n. }	nourishment
ALIMÓNIA, alimóniae, f. }	
ALIQUÁNTULUM, adv.	somewhat, a little
ÁLIQUIS, áliquid, pron. and adj.	{ 1. someone, something, anyone
	{ 2. some
ÁLIUS, ália, áliud (gen. álius), pron. and adj.	other, another, different, else
ALLELÚIA (Hebrew)	'praise ye the Lord'
ALMUS, alma, almum, adj.	kind, nourishing, bountiful
ALO, álere, álui, álitum, 3	to nourish, support, sustain
ALTÁRE, altáris, n.	altar
ALTER, áltera, álterum (gen. altérius), pron. and adj.	one; the other (of two)
ALTUS, alta, altum, adj.	high, deep
ÁMBIGO, ambígere, —, —, 3	to wander about, doubt, waver
ÁMBITUS, ámbitus, m.	a walking round, circle, circumference
AMBO, ambae, ambo, num. adj.	both, two
ÁMBULO, ambuláre, ambulávi, ambulátum, 1	to walk
AMEN (Hebrew)	'so be it'
AMÍTTO, amíttere, amísi, amíssum, 3	to let go, pardon, forgive
AMO, amáre, amávi, amátum, 1	to love
AMOR, amóris, m.	love
AMÓVEO, amovére, amóvi, amótum, 2	to put aside, turn away, remove
AMPLÉCTOR, amplécti, ampléxus, 3 dep.	to embrace

AMPLÍFICO, amplificáre, amplificávi, amplificátum, 1	to extend, enlarge, increase
ÁMPLIUS, comp. adv.	longer, further, more thoroughly
ANCÍLLA, ancíllae, f.	handmaid
ANGÉLICUS, angélica, angélicum, adj.	angelic, of the angels
ÁNGELUS, ángeli, m.	angel
ÁNGULUS, ánguli, m.	corner
ANGÚSTIAE, angustiárum, f. plur.	distresses, tribulations
ÁNIMA, ánimae, f.	soul (irreg. dat. and abl. pl: animábus)
ÁNIMAL, animális, n.	living creature
ANIMÓSUS, animósa, animósum, adj.	bold, full of courage
ÁNIMUS, ánimi, m.	mind
ANNÚNTIO, annuntiáre, annuntiávi, annuntiátum, 1	to proclaim
ANNUS, anni, m.	year
ÁNNUUS, ánnua, ánnuum, adj.	yearly, annual
ANTE (+ acc.), prep.	before, in front of
ÁNTEQUAM, adv.	before
ANTÍQUUS, antíqua, antíquum, adj.	old
ANTÍSTES, antístitis, m.	bishop
APÉRIO, aperíre, apérui, apértum, 4	to open
APOSTÓLICUS, apostólica, apostólicum, adj.	apostolic
APÓSTOLUS, apóstoli, m.	apostle
APPÁREO, apparére, appárui, appáritum, 2	to appear
ÁPPETO, appétere, appetívi, appetítum, 3	to hunger after, pursue
APPROPÍNQUO, appropinquáre, appropinquávi, appropinquátum, 1	to approach
APTO, aptáre, aptávi, aptátum, 1	to prepare, make fit for
APTUS, apta, aptum, adj.	fit, prepared
APUD (+ acc.), prep.	in the presence of
AQUA, aquae, f.	water
ÁQUILA, áquilae, f.	eagle
ARA, arae, f.	raised structure, altar
ARCÁNUS, arcána, arcánum, adj.	secret, hidden
ARCHÁNGELUS, archángeli, m.	archangel
ARCHITRICLÍNUS, architriclíni, m.	chief steward
ARCUS, arcus, m.	bow, rainbow
ÁRIDUS, árida, áridum, adj.	dry, arid
ÁRIES, aríetis, m.	ram
ARVUS, arva, arvum, adj.	ploughed
ASCÉNDO, ascéndere, ascéndi, ascénsum, 3	to go up
ASCÉNSIO, ascensiónis, f.	ascension, going up
ASCRÍBO, ascríbere, ascrípsi, ascríptum, 3	to ascribe, attribute
ASPÉCTUS, aspéctus, m.	vision, countenance
ASPER, áspera, ásperum, adj.	sharp, rough
ASPÉRGO, aspérgere, aspérsi, aspérsum, 3	to sprinkle
ASPÉRNOR, aspernári, aspernátus, 1 dep.	to disdain, reject
ASPÍCIO, aspícere, aspéxi, aspéctum, 5	to look at, face towards
ASPIS, áspidis, f.	asp, adder
ÁSSEQUOR, ássequi, assecútus, 3 dep.	to attain to, obtain
ÁSSERO, assérere, assérui, assértum, 3	to declare, assert
ASSÉRTOR, assertóris, f.	deliverer, restorer of liberty
ASSÚMO, assúmere, assúmpsi, assúmptum, 3	1. to take on 2. to take up
ASTO, astáre, ástiti, ástitum, 3	to stand near, or by
ATQUE, conj.	and
ÁTRIUM, átrii, n.	court, hall
ATTÓLLO, attóllere, —, —, 3	to lift up, raise on high
AUCTOR, auctóris, m.	originator, creator
AÚDEO, audére, ausus sum, 2 semi-dep.	to dare, be bold
AÚDIO, audíre, audívi, audítum, 4	to hear, listen to
AUDÍTIO, auditiónis, f.	report, rumour
AÚFERO, aúferre, ábstuli, ablátum, irreg.	to take away
AÚGEO, augére, auxi, auctum, 2	to increase

AULA, aulae, f.	dwelling, temple, court (of a palace)
AURIS, auris, f.	ear
AURUM, auri, n.	gold
AUTEM, conj.	but, however
AUXÍLIUM, auxílii, n.	help
AVE, AVÉTE (imper. of áveo: other parts of the verb not used)	hail
AVÉRTO, avértere, avérti, avérsum, 3	to turn away
ÁZYMA, azymórum, n.pl.	unleavened bread
BÁCULUM, báculi, n. }	staff, rod
BÁCULUS, báculi, m. }	
BAPTÍSMUS, baptísmi, m. }	baptism
BAPTÍSMA, baptísmatis, n. }	
BAPTÍZO, baptizáre, baptizávi, baptizátum, 1	to baptise
BARBA, barbae, f.	beard
BASILÍSCUS, basilísci, m.	reptile, snake, basilisk
BEATITÚDO, beatitúdinis, f.	blessedness, happiness
BEÁTUS, beáta, beátum, adj.	blessed
BENE, adv.	well
BENEDÍCO, benedícere, benedíxi, benedíctum, 3	to bless
BENEDÍCTIO, benedictiónis, f.	blessing
BENEDÍCTUS, benedícta, benedíctum, adj.	blessed
BENEFÍCIUM, benefícii, n.	benefit
BENEPLÁCITUM, benepláciti, n.	favour, good pleasure
BENÍGNITAS, benignitátis, f.	benevolence, mildness
BENÍGNUS, benígna, benígnum, adj.	benign
BIBO, bíbere, bibi, —, 3	to drink
BLANDUS, blanda, blandum, adj.	smooth, pleasant
BÓNITAS, bonitátis, f.	goodness
BONUS, bona, bonum, adj.	good
BRÁCCHIUM (BRÁCHIUM), brácchii, n.	arm
CADO, cádere, cécidi, casum, 3	to fall
CAELÉSTIS. caeléste, adj. }	heavenly, of heaven
CAÉLICUS, caélica, caélicum, adj. }	
CAÉLITUS, adv.	from heaven
CAELI, caelórum, m. pl.	heaven
CÁLAMUS, cálami, m.	reed, pen
CALIX, cálicis, m.	chalice, cup
CANDOR, candóris, m.	brightness, radiance
CANIS, canis, m. or f.	dog
CANO, cánere, cécini, cantum, 3	to sing
CÁNTICUM, cántici, n.	song
CANTO, cantáre, cantávi, cantátum, 1	to sing
CÁPIO, cápere, cepi, captum, 5	to take, lay hold of, obtain
CAPTÍVITAS, captivitátis, f.	captivity
CAPTÍVUS, captívi, m.	prisoner
CAPTÍVUS, captíva, captívum, adj.	captive, imprisoned
CAPUT, cápitis, n.	head
CÁRITAS, caritátis, f.	love, specifically Divine or Christian love
CARO, carnis, f.	flesh
CARUS, cara, carum, adj.	dear, beloved
CASTRA, castrórum, n.pl.	camp
CASTRA CONSÍSTERE	to encamp (of an army)
CATHÓLICUS, cathólica, cathólicum, adj.	catholic
CAUSA, causae, f.	cause
CEDRUS, cedri, n.b. f.	cedar tree
CELEBRÁTIO, celebratiónis, f.	celebration
CÉLEBRO, celebráre, celebrávi, celebrátum, 1	to celebrate
CELSITÚDO, celsitúdinis, f.	height, exaltation
CENA, cenae, f.	supper
CENO, cenáre, cenávi, cenátum, 1	to have supper, take a meal
CÉNSEO, censére, cénsui, censum, 2	to assess, estimate, think

CÉREUS, cérei, m.	taper, candle
CERNO, cérnere, crevi, cretum, 3	to perceive, discern
CERTO, certáre, certávi, certátum, 1	to strive
CERTUS, certa, certum, adj.	certain, fixed, determined
CERVIX, cervícis, f.	neck
CERVUS, cervi, m.	stag, deer
CESSÁTIO, cessatiónis, f.	a ceasing, stopping
CHORUS, chori, m.	chorus, choir
CHRISTIÁNUS, christiána, christiánum, adj.	Christian
CHRISTUS, Christi, m.	Christ
CIBO, cibáre, cibávi, cibátum, 1	to feed
CIBUS, cibi, m.	food, meat
CINGO, cíngere, cinxi, cinctum, 3	to put on a belt, sword etc.
CIRCÚITUS, circúitus, m.	a circle, a going round (IN CIRCÚITU — round about)
CIRCÚMSTO, circúmstare, circúmsteti, —, 1	to stand around
CÍTHARA, cítharae, f.	stringed instrument, cithara
CIVIS, civis, m. or f.	citizen
CÍVITAS, civitátis, f.	city
CLÁMO, clamáre, clamávi, clamátum, 1	to call, cry out, proclaim
CLAMOR, clamóris, m.	a cry
CLÁRESCO, claréscere, clárui, —, 3	to shine forth
CLARÍFICO, clarificáre, clarificávi, —, 1	to make illustrious or celebrated
CLARITÁS, claritátis, f.	light, brightness, splendour
CLARUS. clara, clarum, adj.	shining, brilliant, illustrious
CLAUDO, claúdere, clausi, clausum, 3	to close
CLAVIS, clavis, f.	key
CLAVUS, clavi, m.	nail
CLEMENS , cleméntis, adj.	clement, gracious, merciful
CLEMÉNTIA, cleméntiae, f.	mercifulness, clemency
CLERUS, cleri, m.	the clergy
COADÚNO, coadunáre, coadunávi, coadunátum, 1	to unite
CO-AETÉRNUS, co-aetérna, co-aetérnum, adj.	co-eternal
COEPI, coepísse, coeptum, 3 defect.	to begin (only perfect form used)
COETUS, coetus, m.	assembly, host
COGITÁTIO, cogitatiónis, f.	thought, reflection, consideration
CÓGITO, cogitáre, cogitávi, cogitátum, 1	to consider thoroughly, meditate upon.
COHÉRES, coherédis, m. or f.	co-heir
COGNÓSCO, cognóscere, cognóvi, cógnitum, 3	to know, understand
COLLAÉTOR, collaetári, collaetátus sum, 1 dep.	to rejoice together
COLLÁTUS, colláta, collátum, adj.	brought together
COLLAUDÁTIO, collaudatiónis, f.	praise
COLLAÚDO, collaudáre. collaudávi, collaudátum, 1	to praise very much
COLLIS, collis, m.	hill
CÓLLOCO, collocáre, collocávi, collocátum, 1	to place
COLO, cólere, cólui, cultum, 3	to worship, reverence, celebrate
COLÚMBA, colúmbae, f.	dove, pigeon
CÓMEDO, comédere, comédi, comésum (coméstum), 3	to eat
CÓMITOR, comitári, comitátus, 1 dep.	to accompany, attend
COMMEMORÁTIO, commemoratiónis, f.	remembrance
COMMÉNDO, commendáre, commendávi, commendátum, 1	to commit, entrust completely
COMMÉRCIUM, commércii, n.	transaction, communication, fellowship
COMMÍTTO, committere, commisi, commíssum, 3	to set, put in place
COMMÍXTIO, commixtiónis, f.	a mixture, mingling
COMMÓVEO, commovére, commóvi, commótum, 2	to shake, disturb greatly
COMMUNICÁTIO, communicatiónis, f.	a communicating, imparting
COMMÚNICO, communicáre, communicávi, communicátum, 1	to share together, have anything in common with
COMMÚNIO, communíre, communívi(ii), commúnitum, 4	to secure, fortify
COMPÁGES, compágis, f.	a joining together, structure
CÓMPARO, comparáre, comparávi, comparátum, 1	to prepare, set in order, arrange

COMPÁTIOR, cómpati, compássus, 3 dep.	to suffer with
COMPETÉNTER, adv.	properly, ably, competently
COMPLÁCEO, complacére, complácui, —, 2	to be pleased, be pleasing (to)
COMPLANTÁTUS, complantáta, complantátum adj.	planted together (in), made level (with)
CÓMPLEO, complére, complévi, complétum, 2	to fulfil, make whole, perfect
COMPLÉTUS, compléta, complétum, adj.	finished
COMPRÓBO, comprobáre, comprobávi, comprobátum, 1	to approve, establish, confirm
COMPÚNGO, compúngere, compúnxi, compúnctum, 3	to pierce
CONCÉDO, concédere, concéssi, concéssum 3	to grant
CONCÉLEBRO, concelebráre, concelebrávi, concelebrátum, 1	to celebrate together with
CONCÍDO, concídere, concídi, concísum, 3	to destroy, divide, cut into small pieces
CONCÍLIO, conciliáre, conciliávi, conciliátum 1	to unite, to make friendly
CÓNCINO, concínere, concínui, —, 3	to sing or play together harmoniously
CONCÍPIO, concípere, concépi, concéptum, 5	to conceive
CONCÓRDIA, concórdiae, f.	agreement, harmony, concord
CONCORS, concórdis, adj.	of the same mind, united
CONCÚLCO, conculcáre, conculcávi, conculcátum, 1	to trample upon, crush, bruise
CONCÚPIO, concúpere, concupívi, concupítum, 5	to desire greatly, long for
CONCUPÍSCO, concupíscere, concupívi, concupítum, 3	to desire, strive after
CONCÚRRO, concúrrere, concúrri, concúrsum, 3	to run together, assemble in a multitude
CONDEMNÁTIO, condemnatiónis, f.	condemnation
CONDÉMNO, condemnáre, condemnávi, condemnátum, 1	to condemn, sentence
CONDÉNSÚS, condénsa, condénsum, adj.	thick, dense, obscure
CONDÍTIO (sometimes CONDÍCIO), conditiónis, f	state, condition
CÓNDITOR, conditóris, m.	founder, establisher
CÓNDITUS, cóndita, cónditum, adj.	made, founded
CONDO, cóndere, cóndidi, cónditum, 3	to put together, establish
CÓNFERO, conférre, cóntuli, collátum, irreg.	to bring together
CONFESSIO confessiónis, f.	confession, praise, acknowledgement
CONFIDÉNTER, adv.	courageously, confidently
CONFÍDO, confídere, confísus sum, 3 semi-dep.	to trust
CONFIGÚRO, configuráre, configurávi, configurátum, 1	to shape, fashion
CONFIRMO, confirmáre, confirmávi, confirmátum. 1	to make firm, establish, strengthen
CONFÍTEOR, confitéri, conféssus sum, 2 dep.	to confess, acknowledge
CONFLÍGO, conflígere, conflíxi, conflíctum, 3	to strive, contend
CONFÓRTO, confortáre, confortávi, confortátum, 1	to strengthen
CONFRÍNGO, confríngere, confrégi, confráctum, 3	to break in pieces
CONFÚGIO, confúgere, confúgi, —, 3	to flee for safety, take refuge
CONFÚNDO, confúndere, confúdi, confúsum, 3	to confound, put to shame
CONGAÚDEO, congaudére, congavísus sum, 2. semi-dep	to rejoice together
CONGLORÍFICO, conglorificáre, conglorificávi, conglorificátum, 1	to glorify together with
CÓNGREGO, congregáre, congregávi, congregátum, 1	to gather together
CONGRUÉNTER, adv.	suitably
CÓNGRUO, congrúere, cóngrui, —, 3	to correspond with, to meet with
CONJUGÁLIS, conjugále, adj.	relating to marriage
CONJÚNGO, conjúngere, conjúnxi, conjúnctum, 3	to unite
CONNÚBIUM, connúbii, n.	marriage, wedlock
CONSCIÉNTIA, consciéntiae, f.	conscience, consciousness, acknowledgement
CONSECRÁTIO, consecratiónis, f.	consecration
CONSÉDEO, consedére, consédi, conséssum, 2	to sit down together (with)
CONSÉRVO, conserváre, conservávi, conservátum, 1	to preserve, keep safe
CÓNSEQUOR, cónsequi, consecútus, 3 dep.	to follow, accompany
CONSÍDERO, consideráre, considerávi, considerátum, 1	to look at closely, examine
CONSÍLIUM, consílii, n.	counsel, deliberation
CONSÍSTO, consístere, cónstiti, cónstitum, 3	{ 1. to take up a position { 2. to rest, remain, endure

CONSOLÁTIO, consolatiónis, f.	consolation
CONSOLÁTOR, consolatóris, m.	consoler
CONSÓLOR, consolári, consolátus, 1 dep. also passive	to comfort, to be comforted
CONSORS, consórtis, adj.	being a sharer, one of a company
CONSORS, consórtis, m. or f.	companion, partaker
CONSÓRTIUM, consórtii, n.	company
CONSPÉCTUS, conspéctus, m.	sight
CONSPÍCIO, conspícere, conspéxi, conspéctum, 3	to look at, observe with attention
CONSPÍCUUS, conspícua, conspícuum, adj.	visible, striking, remarkable
CONSTÍTUO, constítuere, constítui, constitútum, 3	to establish, set in place
CONSTO, constáre, cónstiti, constátum, 1	1. to stand together (with)
	2. to be established, settled, fixed
CONSUBSTANTIÁLIS, consubstantiále, adj. (+ dative)	consubstantial
CONSUMMÁTIO, consummatiónis, f.	perfecting, consummation, end
CONSÚMMO, consummáre, consummávi, consummátum, 1	to accomplish, complete, perfect
CONSÚRGO, consúrgere, consurréxi, consurréctum, 3	to rise together (with)
CÓNTEMPLO, contempláre, contemplávi, contemplátum, 1 CONTÉMPLOR, contemplári, contemplátus, 1 dep. }	to consider, contemplate
CONTÉMPTUS, contémptus, m.	contempt, scorn
CONTÉNDO, conténdere, conténdi, conténtum, 3	to fight, strive
CONTÍNEO, continére, contínui, conténtum, 2	to keep together, preserve
CONTÍNUUS, continua, contínuum, adj.	continuous
CONTRÍSTO, contristáre, contristávi, contristátum, 1	to make sad, afflict
CONTRÍTIO, contritiónis, f.	grief, contrition
CONTRÍTUS, contríta, contrítum, adj.	contrite
CONTÚRBO, conturbáre, conturbávi, conturbátum, 1	to trouble, throw into confusion
CONVENIÉNTER, adv.	suitably, duly
CONVÉNIO, conveníre, convéni, convéntum, 4	to come together
CONVÉNTUS, convéntus, m.	assembly
CONVERSÁTIO, conversatiónis, f.	1. conversation. 2. manner of living, conduct
CONVÉRSO, conversáre, conversávi, conversátum, 1	to change, turn
CONVÉRSOR, conversári, conversátus, 1 dep.	to live with, keep company with
CONVÉRTO, convértere, convérti, convérsum, 3	to turn
CONVÉSCOR, convésci, —, 3 dep.	to eat with (others)
CO-ÓPEROR, co-operári, co-operátus, 1 dep.	to work together with
COPIÓSIUS, comp. adv.	in greater numbers, more abundantly
CÓPULA, cópulae, f.	bond, tie
COR, cordis, n.	heart
CORAM (+ abl.), prep.	in the presence of
CORNU, cornus, n.	horn
CORÓNA, corónae, f.	crown, garland
CORÓNO, coronáre, coronávi, coronátum, 1	to crown
CORPORÁLIS, corporále, adj.	bodily
CORPUS, córporis, n.	body
CORRÍPIO, corrípere, corrípui, corréptum, 3	to reproach, blame
CORRÓBORO, corroboráre, corroborávi, corroborátum, 1	to strengthen greatly, make very strong
CORRÚMPO, corrúmpere, corrúpi, corrúptum, 3 {	1. to destroy, bring to nothing 2. to corrupt, spoil, mar
CORRÚPTIO, corruptiónis, f.	corruption
CORRÚPTUS, corrúpta, corrúptum, adj.	corrupt
CORÚSCO, coruscáre, —, —, 1	to flash, glitter, gleam
COTIDIÁNUS, (sometimes QUOTIDIÁNUS), cotidiána, cotidiánum, adj.	daily
CRÁSTINA DIE, adj. phrase	tomorrow
CREÁTIO, creatiónis, f.	creation
CREATÚRA, creatúrae, f.	creature
CREDO, crédere, crédidi, créditum, 3	to believe
CREO, creáre, creávi, creátum, 1	to create
CRESCO, créscere, crevi, cretum, 3	to grow, arise, be born
CRIMEN, críminis, n.	fault, error, offence
CRUCIFÍGO, crucifígere, crucifixi, crucifíxum, 3	to crucify

CRUX, crucis, f.	cross
CULPA, culpae, f.	fault
CULTOR, cultóris, m. or f.	worshipper, reverencer
CULTUS, cultus, m.	worship
CUM (+ abl.), prep.	with (or as suffix: Dóminus vobiscum)
CUM conj.	when
CÚMULO, cumuláre, cumulávi, cumulátum, 1	to heap up, to fill
CUNCTUS, cuncta, cunctum, adj.	all, whole
CÚPIO, cúpere, cupívi (-ii), cupítum, 5	to desire, delight in
CURA, curae, f.	care, custody
CURRO, cúrrere, cucúrri, cursum, 3	to run, hasten
CURSUS, cursus, m.	course
CUSTÓDIO, custodíre, custodívi, custodítum, 4	to guard, watch over, preserve
DAEMON, daémonis, m. } DAEMÓNIUM, daemónii, n. }	devil, demon
DAMNÁTIO, damnatiónis, f.	damnation
DAPS, dapis, f.	banquet, solemn religious feast
DATOR, datóris, m. or f.	giver
DATUM, dati, n.	gift, thing given
DE (+ abl.), prep.	from, out of
DÉALBO, dealbáre, dealbávi, dealbátum, 1	to make white
DÉBITOR, debitóris, m.	debtor
DÉBITUM, débiti, n.	debt, offence
DECET, decére, décuit, — 2 impers.	it is fitting, proper
DECLÁRO, declaráre, declarávi, declarátum, 1	to signify, reveal
DECOR, decóris, m.	beauty
DECÓRUS, decóra, decórum, adj.	{ 1. beautiful, adorned. 2. fitting, proper
DECUS, décoris, n.	grace, beauty, glory
DEDICÁTIO, dedicatiónis, f.	dedication
DEDÚCO, dedúcere, dedúxi, dedúctum, 3	to lead, bring away
DEFÉNDO, deféndere, deféndi, defénsum, 3	to defend
DEFÉNSIO, defensiónis, f.	defence
DEFÉNSOR, defensóris, m. or f.	defender, protector
DÉFERO, deférre, détuli, delátum, irreg.	to bear, bring forward, offer
DEFÍCIO, defícere, deféci, deféctum, 3	to fail, be lacking in
DEFÚNCTUS, defúncta, defúnctum, adj.	dead
DEFÚNDO, defúndere, defúdi, defúsum, 3	to pour down, pour out
DEÍPARA, Deíparae, f.	Mother of God, God-bearer
DÉITAS, Deitátis, f.	Deity, divine nature
DEJÍCIO, dejícere, dejéci, dejéctum, 3	to lay low
DELÁBOR, delábi, delápsus, 3 dep.	to fail, descend
DELECTAMÉNTUM, delectaménti, n. } DELECTÁTIO, delectatiónis, f. }	delight
DELÉCTO, delectáre, delectávi, delectátum, 1	to delight
DÉLEO, delére, delévi, delétum, 2	to blot out, abolish
DELÍCIAE, deliciárum, n. f. pl.	1. pleasure. 2. favourite, loved object
DELÍCTUM, delícti, n.	sin, dishonour, offence
DELÍNQUO, delínquere, delíqui, delíctum, 3	to do wrong
DEMÓNSTRO, demonstráre, demonstrávi, demonstrátum, 1	to show
DEMUM, adv.	at last
DÉNIQUE, adv.	finally, at length
DÉNUO, adv.	a second time, anew
DEPRECÁTIO, deprecatiónis, f.	prayer, supplication
DÉPRECOR, deprecári, deprecátus, 1 dep.	to pray for, entreat
DEPÚLSO, depulsáre, depulsávi, —, 1.	to drive away, push away
DÉPUTO, deputáre, deputávi, deputátum, 1.	to esteem, reckon
DERELÍNQUO, derelínquere, derelíqui, derelíctum, 3	to abandon, forsake
DESCÉNDO, descéndere, descéndi, descénsum, 3	to come down, descend
DESCÉNSUS, descénsus, m.	descent
DÉSERO, desérere, desérui, desértum, 3	to forsake, abandon

DESÉRTUM, desérti, n.	wilderness
DESÉRVIO, deservíre, —, —, 4	to serve zealously, be devoted to
DESIDERÁNTER, adv.	eagerly
DESIDERÁTUS, desideráta, desiderátum, adj.	desired, longed for
DESÍDERO, desideráre, desiderávi, desiderátum, 1	to long for
DESÍGNO, designáre, designávi, désignátum, 1	to signify, represent
DÉSINO, desínere, desívi (-ii), désitum, 3	to cease
DESÍSTO, desístere, déstiti, déstitum, 3	to stop, cease from
DÉSTRUO, destrúere, destrúxi, destrúctum, 3	to destroy
DESUM, deésse, défui, irreg.	to fail, to be lacking
DÉSUPER, adv.	from above
DETÉRGEO, detergére, detérsi, detérsum, 2	to wipe off, wipe away
DEUS, Dei, m.	God
DEVÍNCO, devíncere, devíci, devíctum, 3	to conquer, overcome
DEVÍTO, devitáre, devitávi, devitátum, 1	to avoid
DÉVIUS, dévia, dévium, adj.	wandering from the way
DEVÓTE, adv.	devotedly
DEVÓTIUS, comp. adv.	more devoutly
DEVÓTIO, devotiónis, f.	devotion
DEXTER, déxtera, déxterum, adj.	right (as opp. to left)
DÉXTERA, déxterae, f.	right hand
DICO, dícere, dixi, dictum, 3	to say
DICTUM, dicti, n.	word
DIES, diéi, m. (but f. when a specific day)	day (TÉRTIA DIE — the third day)
DIFFERÉNTIA, differéntiae, f.	difference
DIFFÚNDO, diffúndere, diffúdi, diffúsum, 3	to pour out, spread out
DIFFÚSUS, diffúsa, diffúsum, adj.	spread out
DIGNÁNTER, adv.	courteously, graciously
DIGNÁTIO, dignatiónis, f.	graciousness
DIGNE, adv.	worthily
DÍGNITAS, dignitátis, f.	dignity, worthiness
DIGNO, dignáre, dignávi, dignátum, 1	to deem worthy
DIGNOR, dignári, dignátus, 1 dep.	to deign, think fit
DIGNUS, digna, dignum, adj. (with abl.)	worthy, suitable
DILÁTO, dilatáre, dilatávi, dilatátum, 1	to enlarge, extend
DILÉCTIO, dilectiónis, f.	love
DILÉCTUS, dilécta, diléctum, adj.	beloved
DÍLIGO, dilígere, diléxi, diléctum, 3	to love, regard above others
DILÚVIUM, dilúvii, n.	flood, deluge
DIMÍTTO, dimíttere, dimísi, dimíssum, 3	1. to forgive. 2. to send away, dismiss
DISCÉDO, discédere, discéssi, discéssum, 3	1. to part from, divide. 2. to go away from
DISCÉRNO, discérnere, discrévi, discrétum, 3	to distinguish
DISCÍPULUS, discípuli, m.	disciple
DISCO, díscere, dídici, —, 3	to learn
DÍSCREPO, discrepáre, discrépui, —, 1	to disagree, to be different
DISCRÉTIO, discretiónis, f.	distinction, separation
DISJÍCIO, disjícere, disjéci, disjéctum, 3	to scatter, disperse
DISJÚNGO, disjúngere, disjúnxi, disjúnctum, 3	to separate, put apart
DISPAR, dísparis, adj.	unequal, different
DISPENSÁTIO, dispensatiónis, f.	dispensation
DISPÉNSO, dispensáre, dispensávi, dispensátum, 1	to regulate, order, direct
DISPÉRSUS, dispérsa, dispérsum, adj.	scattered
DISPLÍCEO, displicére, displícui, displícitum, 2	to displease
DISPÓNO, dispónere, dispósui, dispósitum, 3	to dispose, order
DISPOSÍTIO, dispositiónis, f.	disposition
DISPÓSITOR, dispositóris, m.	disposer, arranger
DISSÍMULO, dissimuláre, dissimulávi, dissimulátum, 1	to pretend, disguise, conceal
DÍSSIPO, dissipáre, dissipávi, dissipátum, 1	to scatter
DISSÓLVO, dissólvere, dissólvi, dissolútum, 3	to dissolve, break up
DITO, ditáre, ditávi, ditátum, 1	to enrich
DIVÉRSITAS, diversitátis, f.	diversity
DIVÉRSUS, divérsa, divérsum, adj.	different, various

DIVES, dívitis, adj.	rich
DÍVIDO, divídere, divísi, divísum, 3	to divide, share out
DIVÍNITAS, divinitátis, f.	divinity, godhead
DIVÍNUS, divína, divínum, adj.	divine
DIVÍTIAE, divitiárum, f. plur.	riches
DO, dare, dedi, datum, irreg.	to give
DÓCEO, docére, dócui, doctum, 2	to teach
DOCTOR, doctóris, m.	teacher
DOCTRÍNA, doctrínae, f.	teaching, knowledge, doctrine
DOCUMÉNTUM, documénti, n.	example, pattern
DOGMA, dógmatis, n.	1. doctrine. 2. decree, order
DÓLEO, dolére, dólui, dólitum, 2	to grieve, mourn
DOLÓSUS, dolósa, dolósum, adj.	deceitful
DOLUS, doli, m.	deceit, fraud
DOMÉSTICUS, doméstica, domésticum, adj.	of the home or household
DOMINÁTIO, dominatiónis, f.	domination, dominion
DOMINÁTOR, dominatóris, m.	ruler, lord
DOMÍNICA, domínicae, f.	Sunday, the Lord's day
DOMÍNICUS, domínica, domínicum, adj.	of or belonging to the Lord
DÓMINOR, dominári, dominátus, 1 dep.	to rule, have dominion over
DÓMINUS, Dómini, m.	Lord
DOMNE, (voc. only) m.	Sir, father (shortened voc. form of Dóminus)
DOMUS, domus, f. (abl. sing: domo)	house
DONEC, adv.	until
DONO, donáre, donávi, donátum, 1	to bestow
DONUM, doni, n.	gift
DÓRMIO, dormíre, dormívi, dormítum, 4	to sleep
DORSUM, dorsi, n.	back
DRACO, dracónis, m.	dragon
DÚBITO, dubitáre, dubitávi, dubitátum, 1	to be uncertain, hesitate
DUCO, dúcere, duxi, ductum, 3	to lead
DUÉLLUM, duélli, n.	conflict between two forces
DULCIS, dulce, adj.	sweet
DUM, conj.	while
DUO, duae, duo, num. adj.	two
DUÓDECIM, num. adj. indecl.	twelve
DUODÉNI, duodénae, duodéna, distrib. num. adj.	twelve each, twelve
DUX, ducis, m.	leader, guide
ECCE, demonstr. adv.	behold!
ECCLÉSIA, ecclésiae, f.	church
EDO, édere, edi, essum, 3	to eat, consume
EDO, édere, édidi, éditum, 3	to bring forth
EDÓCEO, edocére, edócui, edóctum, 2	to instruct, teach thoroughly
EFFÉCTUS, effécta, efféctum, adj.	worked out, completed
ÉFFICAX, efficácis, adj.	effectual, powerful
EFFÍCIO, efficere, efféci, efféctum, 5	to accomplish, effect
EFFÚGIO, effúgere, effúgi, effúgitum, 3	to put to flight
EFFÚLGEO, effulgére, effúlsi, —, 2	to shine forth
EFFÚNDO, effúndere, effúdi, effúsum, 3	to shed, pour out
EGÉNUS, egéna, egénum, adj.	poor, needy
ÉGEO, egére, égui, —, 2	to be needy, to suffer want
EGO, mei, pron.	I, me
EGRÉDIOR, égredi, egréssus sum, 3 dep.	to come out of
EJÍCIO, ejícere, ejéci, ejéctum, 5	to cast out, drive out
ELÉCTI, electórum, m. pl.	the elect
ELÉCTUS, elécta, eléctum, adj.	chosen
ELEEMÓSYNA, eleemósynae, f.	alms, almsgiving
ELÉISON (Greek)	'have mercy'
ELEMÉNTA, elementórum, n. pl.	the first principles of things, elements
ÉLEVO, eleváre, elevávi, elevátum, 1	to lift up, raise
ÉLIGO, elígere, elégi, eléctum, 3	to pick out, choose

ELÍMINO, elimináre, eliminávi, eliminátum, 1 — to put an end to
ÉLOQUOR, éloqui, elocútus sum, 3 dep. — to speak out, declare
EMÍTTO, emíttere, emísi, emíssum, 3 — to send out
EMÚNDO, emundáre, emundávi, emundátum, 1 — to cleanse, purify
ENÁRRO, enarráre, enarrávi, enarrátum, 1 — to tell, relate, show forth
ENIM, conj. — for, because
ENÍTOR, eníti, eníxus, 3 dep. — to bring forth
ENÚTRIO, enutríre, enutrívi (-ii), enutrítum, 4 — to nourish, feed, support
EO, ire, ivi (-ii), itum, irreg. — to go
EPÍSCOPUS, epíscopi, m. — bishop
ÉPULOR, epulári, epulátus, 1 dep. — to feast, eat
ERGO, conj. — therefore
ÉRIGO, erígere, eréxi, eréctum, 3 — to raise, set up
ERÍPIO, erípere, erípui, eréptum, 5 — to snatch away, save
ERROR, erróris, m. — a going astray
ERUBÉSCO, erubéscere, erúbui, —, 3 — to be ashamed
ERÚCTO, eructáre, eructávi, eructátum, 1 — to utter, speak of
ERÚDIO, erudíre, erudívi, erudítum, 4 — to instruct, teach
ERUDÍTIO, eruditiónis, f. — instruction, knowledge
ESCA, escae, f. — food
ESSÉNTIA, esséntiae, f. — essence
ESÚRIO, esuríre, esurívi, esurítum, 4 — to be hungry
ET, conj. — and, also
ÉTENIM, conj. — for
ÉTIAM, conj. — also
ETSI, conj. — although
EUCHARÍSTIA, eucharístiae, f. — the Eucharist
EÚGE, interj. — well done! good!
EVÁDO, evádere, evási, evásum, 3 — to escape from
EVANGÉLICUS, evangélica, evangélicum, adj. — of the gospel
EVANGÉLIUM, evangélii, n. — gospel
EVANGELÍZO, evangelizáre, evangelizávi, evangelizátum, 1 — to preach, spread the gospel
EVÉLLO, evéllere, evélli, evúlsum, 3 — to remove, pluck out
EVÉRTO, evértere, evérti, evérsum, 3 — to overthrow, ruin
EX (+ abl.), prep. — from, away from, out of
EXAÚDIO, exaudíre, exaudívi, exaudítum, 4 — to give ear to, hear graciously
EXCÉLSUM, excélsi, n. (usually plural) — a height, heights
EXCÉLSUS, excélsa, excélsum, adj. — high, excellent
ÉXCITO, excitáre, excitávi, excitátum, 1 — to stir up
EXCLÚDO, exclúdere, exclúsi, exclúsum, 3 — to exclude, keep away
EXÉMPLUM, exémpli, n. — example
ÉXEO, exíre, exívi (-ii), éxitum, irreg. — to go out
EXÉRCEO, exercére, exércui, exércitum, 2 — to engage in, keep occupied with
EXÉRCITUS, exércitus, m. — army
EXHÍBEO, exhibére, exhíbui, exhíbitum, 2 — to display, offer to view
EXÍMIUS, exímia, exímium, adj. — distinguished, extraordinary
ÉXITUS, éxitus, m. — departure, end
EXÓRDIUM, exórdii, n. — beginning
EXÓRO, exoráre, exorávi, exorátum, 1 — to obtain by pleading
EXPEDÍTUS, expedíta, expedítum, adj. — free, unimpeded
EXPÉRIOR, experíri, expértus, 4 dep. — to experience
ÉXPETO, expétere, expetívi (expétii), expetítum, 3 — to seek after, long for
EXPIÁTUS, expiáta, expiátum, adj. — atoned, purified, expiated
ÉXPLEO, explére, explévi, explétum, 2 — to fill, fulfil
ÉXPRIMO, exprímere, expréssi, expréssum, 3 — { 1. to form, devise, invent / 2. to express, represent
EXPÚGNO, expugnáre, expugnávi, expugnátum, 1 — to fight against, overthrow
EXPÚRGO, expurgáre, expurgávi, expurgátum, 1 — to cleanse, purge, purify
EXQUÍRO, exquírere, exquisívi, exquisítum, 3 — to seek for, search out diligently
ÉXSEQUOR, éxsequi, exsecútus, 3 dep. — { 1. to follow after, accompany / 2. to carry out, perform

EXSÍSTO, exsístere, éxstiti, éxstitum, 3	to come forth, emerge, appear
EXSPECTÁTIO, exspectatiónis, f.	expectation
EXSPÉCTO, exspectáre, exspectávi, exspectátum, 1	to look forward to
ÉXSTRUO, exstrúere, exstrúxi, exstrúctum, 3	to build, raise, construct
EXSULTÁTIO, exsultatiónis, f.	joy, gladness
EXSÚLTO, exsultáre, exsultávi, exsultátum, 1	to rejoice
EXSÚPERO, exsuperáre, exsuperávi, exsuperátum, 1	to overcome, rise above
EXSÚRGO, exsúrgere, exsurréxi, exsurréctum, 3	to arise, stand up
EXTÓLLO, extóllere, —, —, 3	to lift up, raise
EXTRÉMUM, extrémi, n.	end, farthest part
ÉXUO, exúere, éxui, exútum, 3	to cast off, lay aside
FÁBRICO, fabricáre, fabricávi, fabricátum, 1	to make, build, work
FÁCIES, faciéi, f.	face
FÁCINUS, facínoris, n.	crime, misdeed
FÁCIO, fácere, feci, factum, 5	to make
FACTOR, factóris, m.	maker
FACÚLTAS, facultátis, f.	capability, means
FAMES, famis, f.	hunger, famine, need
FAMÍLIA, famíliae, f.	family
FÁMULA, fámulae, f.	handmaid
FÁMULO, famuláre, famulávi, —, 1	to use as a servant
FÁMULUS, fámuli, m.	servant
FÁTUOR, fatuári, —, —, 2 dep.	to be inspired
FÁVEO, favére, favi, fautum, 2	to be favourable towards
FAVOR, favóris, m.	favour, approval
FAVUS, favi, m.	honeycomb
FECÚNDITAS, fecunditátis, f.	fruitfulness
FECÚNDUS, fecúnda, fecúndum, adj.	fruitful
FEL, fellis, n.	gall
FELÍCITER, adv.	happily, favourably
FELIX, felícis, adj.	happy, fortunate
FÉMINA, féminae, f.	woman
FERMÉNTUM, ferménti, n.	leaven
FERO, ferre, tuli, latum, irreg.	to carry, bear, bring
FESTUM, festi, n.	festival
FESTÍNO, festináre, festinávi, festinátum, 1	to hasten
FESTÍVITAS, festivitátis, f.	festival
FIDÉLES, fidélium, m. and f. pl.	the faithful
FIDÉLIS, fidéle, adj.	faithful, believing
FIDÉLITER, adv.	faithfully
FIDES, fídei, f.	faith
FIGÚRA, figúrae, f.	form, pre-figuring, type
FIGÚRO, figuráre, figurávi, figurátum, 1	to form, shape
FÍLIA, filiae, f	daughter
FÍLIUS, filii, m	son
FIO, fíeri, factus sum (passive of FÁCIO), irreg.	to become, to be made
FIRMAMÉNTUM, firmaménti, n.	the firmament
FÍRMITER, adv.	firmly, strongly
FIRMO, firmáre, firmávi, firmátum, 1	to strengthen
FLECTO, fléctere, flexi, flexum, 3	to bend
FLEO, flere, flevi, fletum, 3	to weep, lament
FLETUS, fletus, m.	weeping
FLÓREO, florére, flórui, -, 2	to blossom
FLUMEN, flúminis, n.	river
FOEDUS, foéderis, n.	agreement, covenant
FONS, fontis, m.	fountain, spring
FORAS, adv.	out, forth, out of doors
FORE (irreg. future infinitive of SUM)	to be (in the future)
FORIS, adv.	outwardly, outside
FORMA, formae, f.	shape, form
FORMÍDO, formidáre, formidávi, formidátum, 1	to dread, be afraid of

FORMO, formáre, formávi, formátum, 1	to shape, form
FORTITÚDO, fortitúdinis, f.	strength, power
FÓVEO, fovére, fovi, fotum, 2	to warm
FRÁCTIO, fractiónis, f.	a breaking
FRAGÍLITAS, fragilitátis, f.	frailty
FRANGO, frángere, fregi, fractum, 3	to break
FRATER, fratris, m.	brother
FRATÉRNUS, fratérna, fratérnum, adj.	brotherly
FREMO, frémere, frémui, frémitum, 3	to rage, roar
FREQUÉNTIA, frequéntiae, f.	multitude, throng, large number
FREQUÉNTO, frequentáre, frequentávi, frequentátum, 1	to frequent, resort to frequently
FRÍGIDUS, frígida, frígidum, adj.	cold
FRUCTUS, fructus, m.	fruit
FRUGES, frugum, f. plur.	fruits of the earth
FRUÍTIO, fruitiónis, f.	having the use and enjoyment of a thing
FRUMÉNTUM, fruménti, n.	corn
FÚGIO, fúgere, fugi, fúgitum, 3	to flee
FÚLGEO, fulgére, fulsi, -, 2	to shine, lighten
FUNDO, fundáre, fundávi, fundátum, 1	to found, lay the foundations of
FUTÚRUS, futúra, futúrum, adj.	that which is to come
GAÚDEO, gaudére, gavísus sum, 2 semi-dep.	to rejoice
GAÚDIUM, gaúdii, n.	joy
GENERÁTIO, generatiónis, f.	generation
GÉNETRIX, genetrícis, f.	mother
GÉNIMEN, geníminis, n.	fruit, product
GENO, génere, génui, génitum, 3	to beget
GENS, gentis, f.	a people
GENUS, géneris, n.	kind, race, nation
GÉRMINO, germináre, germinávi, germinátum, 1	to put forth, bud
GERO, gérere, gessi, gestum, 3	{ 1. to do, celebrate, accomplish { 2. to carry, bear
GESTO, gestáre, gestávi, gestátum, 1	to carry
GLÁDIUS, gládii, m.	sword
GLÓRIA, glóriae, f.	glory
GLORIFICÁTIO, glorificatiónis, f.	glorification
GLORÍFICO, glorificáre, glorificávi, glorificátum, 1	to glorify
GLÓRIOR, gloriári, gloriátus sum, 1 dep.	to glory in, boast of
GLORIÓSUS, gloriósa, gloriósum, adj.	glorious
GRANUM, grani, n.	grain
GRÁTIA, grátiae, f.	grace: In plural (GRÁTIAE, gratiárum) = thanks
GRATULÁTIO, gratulatiónis, f.	a rejoicing, show of joy
GRÁTULOR, gratulári, gratulátus sum, 1 dep	to rejoice
GRATUS, grata, gratum, adj.	agreeable, gracious, thankful
GRAVIS, grave, adj.	heavy, burdensome, painful
GRESSUS, gressus, m.	step, course, way
GREX, gregis, m.	flock
GUBERNÁCULA, gubernaculórum, n. pl.	guidance, direction, government
GUBÉRNO, gubernáre, gubernávi, gubernátum, 1	to govern, direct
GUSTO, gustáre, gustávi, gustátum, 1	to taste, have a little to eat
HÁBEO, habére, hábui, hábitum, 2	to have BENE HÁBEO = to be well, enjoy good health
IIABITÁCULUM, habitáculi, n.	dwelling, house
HABITÁTIO, habitatiónis, f.	dwelling, habitation
HERÉDITAS, hereditátis, f.	inheritance
HERI, adv.	yesterday
HIC, adv.	here
HIC, haec, hoc, adj. and pron.	this, this thing, this person
HÓDIE, adv.	today
HODIÉRNUS, hodiérna, hodiérnum, adj.	of today, present

HOLOCAÚSTUM, holocaústi, n.	burnt-offering
HOMO, hóminis, m.	man, mankind
HONOR, honóris, m..	honour
HORA, horae, f.	hour, time
HÓRREUM, hórrei, n.	store-house, barn
HORTAMÉNTUM, hortaménti, n.	encouragement
HOSÁNNA (Hebrew)	a shout of praise, appeal for deliverance: 'save now!'
HOSPES, hóspitis, m.	guest
HÓSTIA, hóstiae, f.	victim
HOSTIS, hostis, m. or f.	enemy
HUMÁNITAS, humanitátis, f.	humanity
HÚMERUS, húmeri, m.	shoulder
HUMÍLITAS, humilitátis, f.	humility
HÝDRA, hýdriae, f.	water-jar, water-pot
HYMNUS, hymni, m.	hymn
HYSSÓPUM, hyssópi, n.	hyssop
IDEM, adv.	likewise
IDEM, éadem, idem, pron. and adj.	the same
ÍDEO, adv.	therefore
ÍGITUR, adv.	therefore
ÍGNEUS, ígnea, ígneum, adj.	burning, fiery
IGNIS, ignis, m.	fire
IGNÓSCO, ignóscere, ignóvi, ignótum, 3	to forgive
ILLE, illa, illud, pron. and adj.	that, he, she, it
ILLIBÁTUS, illibáta, illibátum, adj.	unblemished
ILLUC, adv.	there, to that place
ILLUCÉSCO, illucéscere, illúxi, -, 3	to grow light, to dawn
ILLUMINÁTIO, illuminatiónis, f	light
ILLÚMINO, illumináre, illuminávi, illuminátum, 1	to give light, light up
ILLUSTRÁTIO, illustratiónis, f.	brightness
ILLÚSTRO, illustráre, illustrávi, illustrátum, 1	to light up, make clear
IMA, adv.	to or from the depths
IMÁGO, imáginis, f.	image, likeness
ÍMBUO, imbúere, ímbui, imbútum, 3	to fill, nourish, instruct
IMITÁTIO, imitatiónis, f.	imitation
IMITÁTOR, imitatóris, m. } IMITÁTRIX, imitatrícis, f. }	one who imitates
ÍMITOR, imitári, imitátus sum, 1 dep.	to imitate
IMMACULÁTUS, immaculáta, immaculátum, adj.	immaculate, unblemished
IMMÉNSUS, imménsa, imménsum, adj.	unmeasured, boundless, vast
IMMO, adv.	on the contrary
IMMOLÁTIO, immolatiónis, f.	an offering up in sacrifice
ÍMMOLO, immoláre, immolávi, immolátum, 1	to offer in sacrifice
IMMORTÁLITAS, immortalitátis, f.	immortality
IMMÚNDUS, immúnda, immúndum, adj.	unclean
IMPÉDIO, impedíre, impedívi, impedítum, 4	to hinder, impede
IMPÉRIUM, impérii, n	reign, dominion, government
ÍMPERO, imperáre, imperávi, imperátum, 1	to rule over
IMPÍETAS, impietátis, f.	irreverence, impiety
ÍMPIUS, ímpia, ímpium, adj.	wicked, godless
ÍMPLEO, implére, implévi, implétum, 2	to fill, fulfil
IMPLÓRO, imploráre, implorávi, implorátum, 1	to implore, call upon for aid
IMPÓNO, impónere, impósui, impósitum, 3	to put, place lay on
IMPROPÉRIUM, impropérii, n.	reproach
IMPUGNÁTIO, impugnatiónis, f.	attack, assault
IN, prep. + abl.	in, on, at
+ acc.	into
	IN PRIMIS (prep. phrase) = in the first place
INACCESSÍBILIS, inaccessíbile, adj.	unapproachable, inaccessible
INAEQUÁLIS, inaequále, adj.	uneven, differing

INÁNIS, ináne, adj.	empty, vain
INCARNÁTIO, incarnatiónis, f.	incarnation
INCÁRNO, incarnáre, incarnávi, incarnátum, 1	to make flesh
INCÁRNOR, incarnári, incarnátus (passive)	to be made flesh
INCÉDO, incédere, incéssi, incéssum, 3	go, go in, or along
INCÉNSUM, incénsi, n.	incense
INCESSÁNTER, adv.	unceasingly
INCHO, incoháre, incohávi, incohátum, 1	to begin, lay the foundation of
INCLÍNO, inclináre, inclinávi, inclinátum, 1	to incline, bend
ÍNCLITUS, ínclita, ínclitum, adj.	renowned, glorious
INCOLÁTUS, incolátus, m.	a living in, dwelling in, a place
INCÓLUMIS, incólume, adj.	safe, uninjured
INCOLÚMITAS, incolumitátis, f.	safety
INCORRUPTÍBILIS, incorruptíbile, adj.	incorruptible
INCRÉDULUS, incrédula, incrédulum, adj.	unbelieving
INCREMÉNTUM, increménti, n.	growth, increase
INCÚMBO, incúmbere, incúbui, incúbitum, 3	to settle on, make one's home in
INCÚRSIO, incursiónis, f.	attack
INDE, adv.	thence, from there
INDÉBITE, adv.	without just cause, unduly
INDEFÉSSUS, indeféssa, indeféssum, adj.	untiring
INDEFÍCIENS, indeficiéntis, adj.	unfailing
INDESINÉNTER, adv.	unceasingly
INDIVÍDUUS, indivídua, indivíduum, adj. }	
INDIVÍSUS, indivísa, indivísum, adj. }	undivided
INDO, índere, índidi, índitum, 3	to put into, infuse, inspire
INDÚCO, indúcere, indúxi, indúctum, 3	to lead
INDULGÉNTIA, indulgéntiae, f.	pardon, forgiveness
INDÚLGEO, indulgére, indúlsi, indúltum, 2	to grant
ÍNDUO, indúere, índui, indútum, 3	to put on, to be clothed with
INÉBRIO, inebriáre, inebriávi, inebriátum, 1	to make drunk, inebriate
INEFFÁBILIS, ineffábile, adj.	unutterable
INEFFABÍLITER, adv.	unutterably
ÍNEO, iníre, inívi (ínii), ínitum, irreg.	to enter upon, undertake
INESTIMÁBILIS, inestimábile, adj.	
(sometimes spelt INAESTIMÁBILIS)	incalculable, priceless
INFANS, infántis, m. or f.	baby, infant
ÍNFERI, inferórum, n. plur.	1. the dead 2. the underworld, hell
INFÉRNUM, inférni, n.	hell
ÍNFERO, inférre, íntuli, illátum, irreg.	to carry in, bring in
INFINÍTUS, infiníta, infinítum, adj.	infinite
INFÍRMO, infirmáre, infirmávi, infirmátum, 1	to weaken
INFÚNDO, infúndere, infúdi, infúsum, 3	to pour into
INGENS, ingéntis, adj.	great, vast
INGRÉDIOR, íngredi, ingréssus sum, 3 dep.	to enter
INHÁBITO, inhabitáre, inhabitávi, inhabitátum, 1	to live in
INHAÉREO, inhaerére, inhaési, inhaésum, 2	to cleave to, cling to
INIMÍCUS, inimíci, m.	enemy (personal enemy)
INÍQUITAS, iniquitátis, f.	iniquity
INÍQUUS, iníqua, iníquum, adj.	unjust
INÍTIUM, inítii, n.	beginning
INNÍTOR, inníti, innísus (inníxus), 3 dep.	to rest upon, rely on
ÍNNOCENS, innocéntis, adj.	innocent
INNOCÉNTIA, innocéntiae, f.	innocence
INNOTÉSCO, innotéscere, innótui, —, 3	to become known
INNOVÁTIO, innovatiónis, f.	a renewing
INNÓXIUS, innóxia, innóxium, adj.	harmless, innocent
INNÚMERUS, innúmera, innúmerum, adj.	numberless, countless
INOBOEDIÉNTIA, inoboediéntiae, f.	disobedience
INOPS, ínopis, adj.	needy, destitute, afflicted
INORDINÁTUS, inordináta, inordinátum, adj.	disordered, irregular
INQUINAMÉNTUM, inquinaménti, n.	stain, filthiness

INQUÍRO, inquírere, inquisívi, inquisítum, 3	to search for, seek after
INSÍDIAE, insidiárum, f. (plur. only)	plot, snare
INSIPIÉNTIA, insipiéntiae, f.	folly, foolishness
INSPIRÁTIO, inspiratiónis, f.	inspiration
INSPÍRO, inspiráre, inspirávi, inspirátum, 1	to inspire, arouse
INSTAÚRO, instauráre, instaurávi, instaurátum, 1	to renew, celebrate afresh
INSTITÚTIO, institutiónis, f.	inauguration, institution
INSTITÚTUM, institúti, n.	institution, purpose, plan
ÍNSTRUO, instrúere, instrúxi, instrúctum, 3	to draw up, make preparations for
ÍNSULA, ínsulae, f.	island
INSÚRGO, insúrgere, insurréxi, insurréctum, 3	to rise up
ÍNTEGER, íntegra, íntegrum, adj.	whole, unimpaired, entire
INTÉGRITAS, integritátis, f.	wholeness, integrity
INTELLÉCTUS, intelléctus, m.	perception, understanding
INTELLIGÉNTIA, intelligéntiae, f.	the understanding, discernment
INTÉLLIGO, intellígere, intelléxi, intelléctum, 3	to perceive, understand
INTEMERÁTUS, intemeráta, intemerátum, adj.	inviolate, undefiled
INTÉNDO, inténdere, inténdi, inténtum, 3	to turn to, incline to
INTÉNTUS, inténta, inténtum, adj.	intent upon, eager
INTER (+ acc), prep.	among
INTERCÉDO, intercédere, intercéssi, intercéssum, 3	to intercede
INTERCÉSSIO, intercessiónis, f.	intercession
INTÉRITUS, intéritus, m.	destruction, ruin
INTÉRIUS, comp. adv.	more inwardly
INTERPÉLLO, interpelláre, interpellávi, interpellátum, 1	to intercede
INTERVÉNIO, interveníre, intervéni, intervéntum, 4	to interpose (on behalf of someone)
ÍNTIMUS, íntima, íntimum, adj.	inmost
ÍNTONO, intonáre, intónui, intonátum, 1	to thunder
INTRA (+ acc.), prep.	within
INTRO, intráre, intrávi, intrátum, 1	to enter
INTRÓEO, introíre, introívi, intróitum, irreg.	to enter
INTÚEOR, intuéri, intúitus sum, 2 dep.	to consider, look at earnestly
INTUS, adv.	inwardly, within
INVÉNIO, inveníre, invéni, invéntum, 4	to find, discover, learn
INVIOLÁTUS, invioláta, inviolátum, adj.	pure, undefiled
INVISÍBILIS, invisíbile, adj.	invisible
ÍNVOCO, invocáre, invocávi, invocátum, 1	to call upon, invoke
INVÓLVO, invólvere, invólvi, involútum, 3	to wrap up, envelop
IPSE, ipsa, ipsum, demonstr. pron. and adj.	himself, herself, itself
IRACÚNDUS, iracúnda, iracúndum, adj. } IRÁTUS, iráta, irátum, adj. }	angry
IRRÁDIO, irradiáre, irradiávi, irradiátum, 1	to illumine, cast light into
IRREPREHENSÍBILIS, irreprehensíbile, adj.	beyond reproach
IRRÍDEO, irridére, irrísi, irrísum, 2	to laugh at
IS, ea, id, pron. and adj.	{ 1. he, she, it { 2. this
ISTE, ista, istud, demonstr. pron.	this, that
ITA, adv.	thus, in this way
ITEM, conj.	also
ITER, itíneris, n.	journey, passage, way
ÍTERUM, adv.	again
JAM, adv.	now
JANUA, jánuae, f.	door, gate
JEJÚNIUM, jejúnii, n.	fasting
JESUS, acc. JESUM, all other cases JESU, m.	Jesus
JÚBEO, jubére, jussi, jussum, 2	to command, bid
JUBILÁTIO, jubilatiónis, f.	a shouting of joy
JÚBILO, jubiláre, jubilávi, jubilátum, 1	to raise a shout of joy
JUCÚNDITAS, jucunditátis, f.	cheerfulness, joy
JUCÚNDUS, jucúnda, jucúndum, adj.	pleasing, delightful
JUDEX, júdicis, m	judge

JUDÍCIUM, judícii, n.	judgement
JÚDICO, judicáre, judicávi, judicátum, 1	to judge
JÚGITER, adv.	continually
JUGUM, jugi, n.	bond of affection, marriage
JUNGO, júngere, junxi, junctum, 3	to unite, bind
JÚNIOR, junióris, m.	young man
JURO, juráre, jurávi, jurátum, 1	to swear, take an oath
JUSTIFICÁTIO, justificatiónis, f.	justification
JUSTÍTIA, justítiae, f.	justice
JUSTUS, justa, justum, adj.	just, right
JUVÉNTUS, juventútis, f.	youth
KÝRIE (Greek) m.	'O Lord'
LÁBIUM, lábii (usually pl.), n.	lip
LABOR, labóris, m.	work
LAC, lactis, n.	milk
LÁCRIMA, lácrimae, f.	tear, weeping
LÁCRIMOR, lacrimári, lacrimátus sum, 1 dep.	to shed tears, weep
LACUS, lacus, m.	deep, still water, lake
LAETÍFICO, laetificáre, laetificávi, laetificátum, 1	to gladden, make joyful
LAETÍTIA, laetítiae, f.	joy
LAETOR, laetári, laetátus sum, 1 dep.	to rejoice
LAETUS, laeta, laetum, adj.	happy, joyful
LAMPAS, lámpadis, f.	light, lamp
LÁNGUEO, languére, langui, -, 2	to be faint or weak
LAPIS, lápidis, m.	stone
LÁQUEUS, láquei, m.	snare, trap
LÁRGIOR, largíri, largítus sum, 4 dep.	to bestow, distribute freely
LÁRGITAS, largitátis, f.	abundance, generosity
LARGÍTOR, largitóris, m.	one who grants
LÁTEO, latére, látui, -, 2	to lie hidden, escape notice
LATUS, láteris, n.	side
LAUDÁBILIS, laudábile, adj.	worthy of praise
LAUDO, laudáre, laudávi, laudátum, 1	to praise
LAUS, laudis, f.	praise
LAVÁCRUM, lavácri, n.	a bath, washing, water of baptism
LAVO, laváre, lavi, lavátum, 1	to wash
LÉCTIO, lectiónis, f.	a reading
LEGÁLIS, legále, adj.	of or belonging to the law
LEO, leónis, m	lion
LEVÁMEN, leváminis, n.	solace, consolation, mitigation
LEVO, leváre, levávi, levátum, 1	to raise
LIBER, libri, m.	book
LIBER, líbera, líberum, adj.	free
LIBERÁTOR, liberatóris, m.	deliverer
LÍBERO, liberáre, liberávi, liberatum, 1	to set free
LIBÉRTAS, libertátis, f.	freedom
LICET, licére, lícuit, lícitum, 2 impers.	it is allowed, permitted
LIGÁTUS, ligáta, ligátum, adj.	bound, tied
LIGNUM, ligni, n.	wood
LINGUA, linguae, f.	{ 1. tongue { 2. language
LÍNIO, liníre, liníví, liníctum, 4	to anoint
LÓCUPLES, locuplétis, adj.	copious, well-provided
LOCUPLÉTO, locupletáre, locupletávi, locupletátum, 1	to enrich
LOCUS, loci, m	place
LONGANÍMITAS, longanimitátis, f.	long-suffering, forbearance
LONGE, adv.	far
LONGITÚDO, longitúdinis, f.	length
LOQUOR, loqui, locútus sum, 3 dep.	to speak
LÚCEO, lucére, luxi, -, 2.	to shine

LUCRIFÁCIO, lucrifácere, lucriféci, 5	to gain, acquire
LÚCIFER, lucíferi, m.	day star, morning star
LÚGEO, lugére, luxi, luctum, 2	to lament, sorrow
LUMEN, lúminis, n.	light
LUNA, lunae, f.	moon
LUTUM, luti, n.	clay
LUX, lucis, f.	light
MÁCULA, máculae, f.	stain, blemish
MAESTUS, maesta, maestum, adj.	sad, sorrowful
MAGIS, adv.	rather
MÁGISTER, mágistri, m.	master
MAGNÁLIA, magnálium, n.pl.	wonders, wonderful works
MAGNÍFICO, magnificáre, magnificávi, magnificátum, 1	to enlarge, magnify, exalt
MAGNUS, magna, magnum, adj.	great
MAGUS, magi, m.	wise man
MAJÉSTAS, majestátis, f.	majesty
MALÍGNITAS, malignitátis, f.	spite, malice
MALÍTIA, malítiae, f.	malice, evil
MALUM, mali, n.	evil
MANDÁTUM, mandáti, n.	commandment
MANDO, mandáre, mandávi, mandátum, 1	to command, commit to one's charge
MANDÚCO, manducáre, manducávi, manducátum, 1	to eat
MANE, adv.	in the morning
MÁNEO, manére, mansi, mansum, 2	to remain
MANIFÉSTO, manifestáre, manifestávi, manifestátum, 1	to show clearly, reveal
MANIFÉSTO or MANIFÉSTE, adv.	clearly, openly
MANIFÉSTUS, manifésta, maniféstum, adj.	clear, manifest
MANNA, n. indecl. or f.	manna
MÁNSIO, mansiónis, f.	a resting-place
MANSUETÚDO, mansuetúdinis, f.	mildness, gentleness
MANUS, manus, f.	hand
MARE, maris, n.	sea
MARGARÍTA, margarítae, f.	pearl
MARITÁLIS, maritále, adj.	of or belonging to marriage, married people
MARTYR, mártyris, m. or f.	martyr
MATER, matris, f.	mother
MÁXIMUS (superlative of MAGNUS), máxima, máximum, adj.	very great, greatest
MEDÉLA, medélae, f.	remedy
MEDIÁTOR, mediatóris, m	mediator
MEDICINÁLIS, medicinále, adj.	medicinal, healing
MÉDITOR, meditári, meditátus sum, 1 dep.	to consider, think about
MÉDIUM, médii, n.	midst, middle
MEL, mellis, n.	honey
MELOS, meli, n.	song, hymn, melody
MEMBRUM, membri, n.	limb, part, member
MÉMINI, meminísse, —, defect. (perfect form)	to remember, be mindful
MEMÓRIA, memóriae, f.	memory
MÉMORO, memoráre, memorávi, memorátum, 1	to be mindful of, call to mind
MEMORIÁLE, memoriális, n.	remembrance, memorial
MENS, mentis, f.	mind
MENSA, mensae, f.	table
MÉNTIOR, mentíri, mentítus sum, 4 dep.	to lie, speak falsely about
MÉREO, merére, mérui, méritum, 2 ⎫ MÉREOR, meréri, méritus sum, 2 dep. ⎭	to deserve
MERIDIÁNUS, meridiána, meridiánum, adj.	of the middle of the day
MÉRITO, meritáre, meritávi, meritátum, 1	to deserve
MÉRITO, adv.	deservedly, justly
MÉRITUM, mériti, n.	1. merit 2. reward, recompense
MEUS, mea, meum, possess. adj.	my

MIGRO, migráre, migrávi, migrátum, 1	to depart, go away
MILÍTIA, milítiae, f.	army
MILLE (pl. míllia), adj. indecl.	thousand
MÍNIMUS, mínima, mínimum, adj. (superlative of PARVUS)	smallest, least
MINÍSTER, minístri, m. ⎫ MINÍSTRA, minístrae, f. ⎭	servant
MINÍSTRO, ministráre, ministrávi, ministrátum, 1	to serve
MÍNUO, minúere, mínui, minútum, 3	to diminish, be lacking
MIRÁBILIS, mirábile, adj.	wonderful
MIRABÍLITER, adv.	wonderfully
MIRÁCULUM, miráculi, n.	miracle, wonder, marvel
MIRÁNDUS, miránda, mirándum, (gerundive of MIROR)	extraordinary, strange
MIRE, adv.	wonderfully, marvellously
MIRÍFICUS, mirífica, miríficum, adj.	wonderful, marvellous
MIROR, mirári, mirátus sum, 1 dep.	to marvel at
MIRUS, mira, mirum, adj.	wonderful
MISERÁTIO, miserationis, f.	mercy, compassion
MISERÁTUS, miseráta, miserátum, adj.	having compassion, mercy
MISÉREOR, miseréri, miséritus sum, (+ gen. or dat.), 2 dep.	to have mercy on
MISERICÓRDIA, misericórdiae, f.	mercy
MISERICÓRDITER, adv.	mercifully
MISÉRICORS, misericórdis, adj.	merciful
MISSA, missae, f.	1. the Mass 2. dismissal
MITIS, mite, adj.	tender, mild
MITTO, míttere, misi, missum, 3	to send
MÓDERO, moderáre, modarávi, moderátum, 1	to set bounds to, regulate
MODÉSTIA, modéstiae, f.	moderation, sober behaviour
MODUS, modi, m.	manner, way
MÓNEO, monére, mónui, mónitum, 2	to admonish, instruct
MONS, montis, m.	mountain
MONUMÉNTUM, monuménti, n.	tomb, sepulchre
MORBUS, morbi, m.	sickness of body or mind
MÓRIOR, mori, mórtuus sum, 3 dep.	to die
MOROR, morári, morátus sum, 1 dep.	to delay
MORS, mortis, f.	death
MORTÁLIS, mortále, adj.	mortal
MORTÁLITAS, mortalitátis, f.	mortality
MÓRTUUS, mórtua, mórtuum, adj.	dead
MOS, moris, m.	⎧ 1 manner, conduct, character ⎩ 2.custom, morals
MÓVEO, movére, movi, motum, 2	⎧ 1. to move, affect, influence ⎩ 2. to quake
MÚLIER, mulíeris, f.	woman
MULSUM, mulsi, n.	wine mixed or made with honey, mead
MULTIFÁRIE, adv.	in many ways
MULTIFÓRMIS, multifórme, adj.	various, diverse
MULTÍPLICO, multiplicáre, multiplicávi, multiplicátum, 1	to multiply, increase
MULTITÚDO, multitúdinis, f.	many, the multitude
MUNDÁNUS, mundána, mundánum, adj.	of or belonging to the world
MUNDÍTIA, mundítiae, f.	cleanness
MUNDO, mundáre, mundávi, mundátum, 1	to cleanse
MUNDUS, mundi, m.	world
MUNDUS, munda, mundum, adj.	clean, cleansed
MÚNIA, n. pl. (nom. + acc. only)	services, duties
MUNÍFICUS, munífica, muníficum, adj.	generous, benevolent
MÚNIO, muníre, munívi, munítum, 4	to strengthen, fortify
MUNUS, múneris, n.	gift, offering, purpose
MUTO, mutáre, mutávi, mutátum, 1	to alter, change
MÚTUUS, mútua, mútuum, adj.	in exchange, mutual

MYRRHA, myrrhae, f.	myrrh
MYSTÉRIUM, mystérii, n.	mystery
MÝSTICE, adv.	mystically
NAM, conj.	for, as, because
NAMQUE, conj	for indeed
NARRO, narráre, narrávi, narrátum, 1	to tell, relate
NASCOR, nasci, natus sum, 3 dep.	to be born
NÁTIO, natiónis, f.	nation
NATÍVITAS, nativitátis, f.	nativity
NATÚRA, natúrae, f.	nature
NAVIS, navis, f.	ship
NE, adv. and conj.	not
NEC, conj.	neither
NECNON, conj.	and also
NECTO, néctere, nexi (néxui), nexum, 3.	to bind, join together
NEGOTIÁTOR, negotiatóris, m.	merchant, trader
NEGÓTIUM, negótii, n.	business, matter, thing
NEMO, néminis, pron.	no-one
NEQUÁNDO, adv.	lest ever
NEQUE, conj.	neither
NÉSCIO, nescíre, nescívi (-ii), nescítum, 4.	not to know, to be ignorant of
NEXO, nexáre, néxui, —, 1.	to bind, join together
NEXUS, nexa, nexum, adj.	bound to, under an obligation to
NIDUS, nidi, m.	nest
NIHIL, n. indecl.	nothing
NIMIS, adv.	very much, too much
NISI, conj.	unless
NIX, nivis, f.	snow
NÓCEO, nocére, nócui, nócitum, 2	to harm, hurt
NOCTÚRNUS, noctúrna, noctúrnum, adj.	of the night, nocturnal
NOLO, nolle, nólui, —, irreg.	to be unwilling
NOMEN, nóminis, n.	name
NÓMINO, nomináre, nominávi, nominátum, 1	to name
NON, adv.	not
NONDUM, adv.	not yet
NOS, nostrum (nostri), pron.	we, us
NOSCO, nóscere, novi, notum, 3	to know, acquire knowledge of
NOSTER, nostra, nostrum, adj.	our
NOTUS, nota, notum, adj.	known
NOVÉLLUS, novélla, novéllum, adj.	new, fresh, young
NOVÍSSIMUS, novíssima, novíssimum, adj. (superlative of NOVUS)	last, final
NÓVITAS, novitátis, f.	newness, freshness
NOVUS, nova, novum, adj.	new
NOX, noctis, f.	night
NÓXIUS, nóxia, nóxium, adj.	harmful
NUBES, nubis, f.	cloud
NUBO, núbere, nupsi, nuptum, 3	to marry, be married to
NULLUS, nulla, nullum, (gen. núllius), adj. and pron.	no, none, no-one
NUMEN, núminis, n.	the divine will, power, presence
NÚMERO, numeráre, numerávi, numerátum, 1	to number
NUMQUAM or NUNQUAM, adv.	never
NUNC, adv.	now
NÚNTIO, nuntiáre, nuntiávi, nuntiátum, 1	to announce, proclaim
NÚNTIUS, núntii, m.	messenger
NÚPTIAE, nuptiárum, f. pl.	marriage, wedding
NÚTRIO, nutríre, nutrívi (-ii), nutrítum, 4	to nourish, feed
O, interj.	Oh!
OBAÚDIO, obaudíre, obaudívi, obaudítum, 4	to cause to be heard
OBDÓRMIO, obdormíre, obdormívi (-ii), obdormítum, 4	to fall asleep
ÓBEO, obíre, obívi, óbitum, 4	to die

OBLÁTIO, oblatiónis, f.	oblation
OBLIVÍSCOR, oblivísci, oblítus sum, 3 dep.	to forget
OBOEDIÉNTIA, oboediéntiae, f.	obedience
OBOÉDIO or OBÉDIO, oboedíre, oboedívi oboédii, oboedítum, 4	to give obedience, to be subject to
OBSCÚRUM, obscúri, n.	darkness, obscurity
OBSÉQUIUM. obséquii. n.	service
OBTÍNEO, obtinére, obtínui, obténtum, 2	to obtain, possess
OBÚMBRO, obumbráre, obumbrávi, obumbrátum, 1	to overshadow
OBUMBRÁTIO, obumbratiónis, f.	shadow, over-shadowing
ÓBVIO, obviáre, obviávi, obviátum, 1	to go towards, meet
ÓBVIUS, óbvia, óbvium, adj.	on the way, meeting
	ÓBVIAM VENÍRE: to come to meet
OCCÁSUS, occásus, m.	setting (of the sun)
OCCÍDO, occídere, occídi, occísum, 3	to kill
OCCÚRRO, occúrrere, occúrri, occúrsum, 3	to run to meet, welcome
OCTO, num. adj. indecl.	eight
ÓCULUS, óculi, m.	eye
ODI, odísse, osus sum, defect. (perfect form)	to hate
ODOR, odóris, m.	odour, scent
OFFÉNDO, offéndere, offéndi, offénsum, 3	{ 1. to strike against, stumble { 2. to displease, offend
ÓFFERO, offérre, óbtuli, oblátum, irreg.	to offer
OFFÍCIUM, officii, n.	service, duty
ÓLEUM, ólei, n.	oil
OLIM, adv.	formerly, once
OLÍVA, olívae, f.	olive, olive-tree or branch
OMÍSSIO, omissiónis, f.	omission
OMNIS, omne, adj.	all, every
OMNÍPOTENS, omnipoténtis, adj.	almighty
ÓNERO, oneráre, onerávi, onerátum, 1	to load, burden
OPE, opis, f. (abl. form; nom. does not occur)	aid, help, support
OPERÁTIO, operatiónis, f.	operation, working
ÓPEROR, operári, operátus sum, 1 dep.	to work for, tend towards
OPÍTULO, opituláre, opitulávi, opitulátum, 1	to help
OPÓRTET, opórtere, opórtuit, 2 impers.	it is necessary
OPPORTÚNUS, opportúna, opportúnum, adj.	suitable, seasonable
OPPRÓBRIUM, oppróbrii, n.	reproach
OPTO, optáre, optávi, optátum, 1	to desire, wish for
OPUS, óperis, n.	work, dead, action
ORBIS, orbis, m.	globe, world
ÓRDINO, ordináre, ordinávi, ordinátum, 1	to set, lay out
ORDO, órdinis, m.	order
ÓRIENS, oriéntis, m.	the east
ORIGINÁLIS, originále, adj.	original
ORÍGO, oríginis, f.	origin
ÓRIOR, oríri, ortus sum, 4 dep.	to arise, become visible
ORNO, ornáre, ornávi, ornátum, 1	to fit out, furnish, dress
ORO, oráre, orávi, orátum, 1	to pray
ÓRPHANUS, órphani, m.	orphan
ORTHODÓXUS, orthodóxa, orthodóxum, adj.	orthodox
ORTUS, ortus, m.	1. rising of the sun. 2. origin
OS, ossis, n.	bone
OS, oris, n.	mouth
OSTÉNDO, osténdere, osténdi, osténsum, 3	to show
ÓSTIUM, óstii, n.	gate
OVIS, ovis, f.	sheep
PÁBULUM, pábuli, n.	food, nourishment
PACÍFICO, pacificáre, pacificávi, pacificátum, 1	to pacify, keep in peace
PACÍFICUS, pacífica, pacíficum, adj.	of peace, peaceful
PALMES, pálmitis, m.	branch

PANGO, pángere, panxi, panctum, 3 — to compose, celebrate, sing
PANIS, panis, m. — bread
PAPA, Papae, m. — Pope
PAR, paris, n. — pair
PAR, paris, adj. — equal, like
PARÁTUS, paráta, parátum, adj. — prepared
PARCO, párcere, péperci, pársum, 3 — to spare, not to injure
PARENS, paréntis, m. or f. — parent
PÁRIO, párere, péperi, partum (páritum), 5 — to bear, to give birth to
PÁRITER, adv. — equally, as well
PARO, paráre, parávi, parátum, 1 — to prepare
PARS, partis, f. — part, lot, portion
PÁRTICEPS, partícipis, m. — sharer
PARTICIPÁTIO, participatiónis, f. — a sharing
PARTÍCIPO, participáre, participávi, participátum, 1 — to have a share in
PARTUS, partus, m. — bringing forth, childbirth
PARVUS, parva, parvum, adj. — small
PASCHÁLIS, paschále, adj. — of Easter, paschal
PASCO, páscere, pavi, pastum, 3 — to feed, nourish
PÁSCUA, páscuae, f. — pasture
PASSER, pásseris, m. — sparrow
PÁSSIO, passiónis, f. — passion, suffering
PASTOR, pastóris, m. — shepherd
PASTUS, pastus, m. — food, sustenance
PATER, patris, m. — father
PATIÉNTIA, patiéntiae, f. — patience
PÁTIOR, pati, passus sum, 3 dep. — to suffer, undergo
PÁTRIA, pátriae, f. — native country
PATRIÁRCHA, patriárchae, m. — patriarch
PATROCÍNIUM, patrocínii, n. — protection, defence, patronage
PAUPER, paúperis, adj. — poor
PAX, pacis, f. — peace
PECCÁTOR, peccatóris, m. — sinner
PECCÁTUM, peccáti, n. — sin
PAUCUS, pauca, paucum, adj. — small in size or in number
PECCO, peccáre, peccávi, peccátum, 1 — to sin
PECTUS, péctoris, n. — breast (figuratively) = heart, feelings, disposition
PELLO, péllere, pépuli, pulsum, 3 — to push, knock, strike
PENETRÁLIS, penetrále, adj. — piercing, penetrating
PÉNETRO, penatráre, penetrávi, penetrátum, 1 — to enter, reach into, penetrate
PENNA, pennae, f. — feather, wing
PER (+ acc.), prep. — through
PÉRAGO, perágere, perégi, peráctum, 3 — to finish, accomplish
PERÁMBULO, perambuláre, parambulávi, perambulátum, 1 — to go around, walk about
PERCÉPTIO, perceptiónis, f. — a receiving, taking in
PERCÍPIO, percípere, percépi, percéptum, 5 — to experience, receive
PERCÚRRO, percúrrere, percúrri, percúrsum, 3 — to run through, run over in one's mind
PÉRDITUS, pérdita, pérditum, adj. — ruined, lost
PERDÚCO, perdúcere, perdúxi, perdúctum, 3 — to lead, bring
PEREGRÍNOR, peregrinári, peregrinátus sum, 1 dep. — to travel on a pilgrimage
PEREGRINÁTIO, peregrinatiónis, f. — journey, pilgrimage
PERÉNNIS, perénne, adj. — eternal
PERÉNNITER, adv. — continually, for ever
PÉREO, períre, perívi (-ii), péritum, irreg. — to be lost, perish, come to nothing
PERFÉCTIO, perfectiónis, f. — perfection
PERFÉCTUS, perfécta, perféctum, adj. — perfect
PÉRFERO, perférre, pértuli, perlátum, irreg. — to carry, convey
PERFÍCIO, perficere, perféci, perféctum, 5 — to make perfect
PÉRFRUOR, pérfrui, perfrúctus sum, 3 dep. — to enjoy thoroughly
PERFÚNDO, perfúndere, perfúdi, perfúsum, 3 — to moisten, sprinkle
PERHÍBEO, perhibére, perhíbui, perhíbitum, 2 — to report, bear witness
PERÍCULUM, perículi, n. — danger

PERLÚSTRO, perlustráre, perlustrávi, perlustrátum, 1	to purify or hallow completely
PERMÁNEO, permanére, permánsi, permánsum, 2	to remain, endure
PERMÍTTO, permíttere, permísi, permíssum, 3	to permit
PERPÉNDO, perpéndere, perpéndi, perpénsum, 3	to weigh carefully, consider
PERPÉTUO, adv.	constantly
PERPÉTUUS, perpétua, perpétuum, adj.	everlasting
PERQUÍRO, perquírere, perquisívi, perquisítum, 3	to make a thorough search, inquire for
PERSECÚTIO, persecutiónis, f.	persecution
PÉRSEQUOR, pérsequi, persecútus sum, 3 dep.	to pursue, harry, persecute
PERSÉVERO, perseveráre, perseverávi, perseverátum, 1	to continue steadily, persevere
PERSÓNA, persónae, f.	person
PERTÍNEO, pertinére, pertínui, perténtum, 2	to reach to, extend
PERTURBÁTIO, perturbatiónis, f.	disquiet, disturbance
PERÚNGO, perúngere, perúnxi, perúnctum, 3	to anoint
PERVÉNIO, perveníre, pervéni, pervéntum, 4	to arrive at, reach
PERVÍGILIS, pervígile, adj.	ever watchful
PES, pedis, m.	foot
PETÍTIO, petitiónis, f.	petition, request
PETO, pétere, petívi (-ii) petítum, 3	to seek, request, beseech
PETRA, petrae, f.	rock, stone
PHASE, n. indecl.	the Passover, the sacrifice offered at the Passover
PIÁCULUM, piáculi, n.	sin, offence, guilt
PÍETAS, pietátis, f.	tenderness, compassion, goodness
PIGNUS, pígnoris, n.	pledge, security
PÍNGUIA, n.pl.	fat meats
PINGUIS, pingue, adj.	fat, rich, fertile
PISCÁTOR, piscatóris, m.	fisherman
PIUS, pia, pium, adj.	merciful, tender, devout
PLACÁTIO, placatiónis, f.	a soothing, propitiation
PLACÁTUS, placáta, placátum, adj.	pleased, placated, appeased
PLÁCEO, placére, plácui, plácitum, 2	to please, be pleasing
PLANTO, plantáre, plantávi, plantátum, 1	set, plant, fix in place
PLAUDO, plaúdere, plausi, plausum, 3	to clap
PLEBS, plebis, f.	a people, the people
PLENITÚDO, plenitúdinis, f.	fullness
PLENUS, plena, plenum, adj.	full
PLORO, ploráre, plorávi, plorátum, 1	to weep, lament
PLUO, plúere, pluvi, -, 3	to rain
PLÚRIES, adv.	often
POENA, poenae, f.	punishment, pain
PONDUS, pónderis, n.	weight, burden
PONO, pónere, pósui, pósitum, 3	to place, appoint, lay down
PÓPULUS, pópuli, m.	people
PORTA, portae, f.	gate
PORTO, portáre, portávi, portátum, 1	to carry
POSCO, póscere, popósci, - 3	to beg, ask for urgently
PÓSITUS, pósita, pósitum, adj.	placed
POSSÉSSIO, possessiónis, f.	possession
POSSÍDEO, possidére, possédi, posséssum, 2	to possess
POSSUM, posse, pótui, irreg.	to be able
POST (+ acc.), prep. and adv.	after
PÓSTULO, postuláre, postulávi, postulátum, 1	to ask
POSTQUAM, conj.	after, as soon as
POTENS, poténtis, adj.	powerful
POTENTÁTUS, potentátus, m.	might, power
POTÉNTER, adv.	powerfully, mightily
POTÉNTIA, poténtiae, f. ⎫ POTÉSTAS, potestátis, f. ⎭	power
POTÍSSIMUM, adv.	chiefly, especially
PÓTIUS, comp. adv.	rather, by preference
POTO, potáre, potávi, potátum, 1	to drink, give to drink
POTUS, potus, m.	drink

PRAE (+ abl.), prep. 　 { 1. in the sight of
　 2. because of

PRAÉBEO, praebére, praébui, praébitum, 2 　 to grant, offer

PRAECÉDO, praecédere, praecéssi, praecéssum, 3 　 to go before

PRAECÉPTUM, praecépti, n. 　 precept, instruction

PRAECÍNGO, praecíngere, praecínxi, praecínctum, 3 　 to gird about

PRAECÍPUUS, praecípua, praecípuum, adj. 　 particular, special

PRAECLÁRUS, praeclára, praeclárum, adj. 　 excellent

PRAECÓNIUM, praecónii, n. 　 a proclaiming, crying out in public

PRAECÚRRO, praecúrrere, praecúrri, praecúrsum, 3 　 { 1. to run before
　 2. to take precedence over

PRAECÚRSOR, praecursóris, m. 　 forerunner, precursor

PRAEDICÁTIO, praedicatiónis, f. 　 preaching, proclaiming

PRAÉDICO, praedicáre, praedicávi, praedicátum 1 　 to proclaim, make publicly known

PRAEDÍCO, praedícere, praedíxi, praedíctum, 3 　 to foretell, predict

PRAEFIGÚRO, praefiguráre, praefigurávi, praefigurátum, 1 　 to prefigure

PRAEFÚLGEO, praefulgére, praefúlsi, —, 2 　 to shine in front of

PRAÉMIUM, praémii, n. 　 reward

PRAEPARÁTIO, praeparatiónis, f. 　 preparation

PRAÉPARO, praeparáre, praeparávi, praeparátum, 1 　 to prepare

PRAESENS, praeséntis, adj. 　 present

PRAESÉNTIA, praeséntiae, f. 　 presence

PRAESÉNTO, praesentáre, praesentávi, —, 1 　 to show, present, hold

PRAESÉPE, praesépis, n. 　 crib, manger

PRAESÍDIUM, praesídii, n. 　 defence

PRAESÍGNO, praesignáre, praesignávi, praesígnátum, 1 　 to make before, prefigure

PRAESTO, praestáre, praéstiti, praéstitum, 1 　 go, give, grant, bestow

PRAESTÓLOR, praestolári, praestolátus, 1 dep. 　 to stand ready for, expect

PRAETÉNDO, praeténdere, praeténdi, praeténtum, 3 　 to stretch or extend towards

PRAETER, adv. 　 { 1. except
　 2. beyond, above

PRAETEREÚNTIA praetereuntiórum, n.pl. 　 passing things (of this world)

PRAETÉRITUS, praetérita, praetéritum, adj. 　 past

PRAEVÁLEO, praevalére, praeválui, —, 2 　 to have greater power, gain the upper hand

PRAEVÉNIO, praeveníre, praevéni, praevéntum, 4 　 to come before

PRAÉVIUS, praévia, praévium, adj. 　 going before, preceding

PRÁNDEO, prandére, prandi, pransum, 2 　 to eat early in the day, take breakfast

PRECES, precum, f.plur. 　 prayers

PRECOR, precári, precátus, 1 dep. 　 to request, beseech, pray

PRETIÓSUS, pretiósa, pretiósum, adj. 　 of great price, precious

PRÍDIE, adv. 　 on the day before

PRIMÍTIAE, primitiárum, f.plur. 　 first things, first fruits, first people

PRIMITÍVUS, primitíva, primitívum, adj. 　 in its early stages

PRIMUM, adv. 　 at first, in the beginning

PRIMUS, prima, primum, adj. 　 first
　 IN PRIMIS: in the first place, first of all

PRINCEPS, príncipis, m. 　 prince, ruler, head

PRINCIPÁLITER, adv. 　 chiefly, mainly

PRINCÍPIUM, princípii, n. 　 beginning

PRIUS, comp. adv. 　 before, sooner

PRIÚSQUAM, adv. 　 before

PRO (+ abl.), prep. 　 for

PROBO, probáre, probávi, probátum, 1 　 to try, test, examine

PROCÉDO, procédere, procéssi, procéssum, 3 　 to come forth

PRÓCIDO, procídere, prócidi, —, 3 　 to fall down, prostrate oneself

PROCLÁMO, proclamáre, proclamávi, proclamátum, 1 　 to cry out, proclaim

PRÓDEO, prodíre, prodívi (-ii), próditum, irreg. 　 to appear, emerge

PROÉLIUM, proélii, n. 　 battle

PRÓFERO, proférre, prótuli, prolátum, irreg. 　 to bring out, lay before, display

PROFÍCIO, proficere, proféci, proféctum, 5 　 to avail, advance

PROFÍTEOR, profitéri, proféssus sum, 2 dep. 　 to profess, acknowledge

PROFÚNDO, profúndere, profúdi, profúsum, 3 　 to pour out, cause to flow

PROFÚNDUS, profúnda, profúndum, adj. 　 deep

PROGÉNIES, progeniéi, f.	lineage, descendants
PROLES, prolis, f.	offspring
PROLÓNGO, prolongáre, prolongávi, prolongátum 1	to prolong, extend
PROMÍSSIO, promissiónis, f.	promise
PROMÍTTO, promíttere, promísi, promíssum, 3	to promise
PROMO, prómere, prompsi, promptum, 3	to bring out, produce, utter
PROMPTE, adv.	readily, quickly
PRONÚNTIO, pronuntiáre, pronuntiávi, pronuntiátum, 1	to proclaim, announce
PROPAGÁTOR, propagatóris, m.	one who extends, enlarges
PROPE, adv.	near
PROPÉNSIUS, comp. adv.	more readily, more willingly
PROPHÉTA, prophétae, m.	prophet
PROPÍNQUO, propinquáre, propinquávi, propinquátum, 1	to approach, attain
PROPÍNQUUS, propínqua, propínquum, adj.	1. near. 2. next of kin
PROPÍTIO, propitiáre, propitiávi, propitiátum, 1	to appease, make favourite
PROPÍTIUS, propítia, propítium, adj.	favourable, gracious
PROPÓNO, propónere, propósui, propósitum, 3	to put forward, set out
PROPRÍETAS, proprietátis, f.	particular quality, distinction
PRÓPRIUS, própria, próprium, adj.	special, particular, one's own
PROPTER (+ acc.), prep. and adv.	on account of, for the sake of
PROPTÉREA, adv.	therefore
PRÓSEQUOR, prósequi, prosecútus sum, 3 dep.	to honour, regard, attend upon
PROSUM, prodésse, prófui, irreg.	to be useful, to benefit
PROTÉCTIO, protectiónis, f.	protection
PROTÉCTOR, protectóris, m.	protector
PRÓTEGO, protégere, protéxi, protéctum, 3	to protect, defend
PROVÉCTIO, provectiónis, f.	advancement, progress
PRÓVEHO, provéhere, provéxi, provéctum, 3	to lead on
PROVÉNIO, proveníre, provéni, provéntum, 4	{ 1. to come forth, appear { 2. to prosper, flourish
PROVÍDEO, providére, provídi, provísum, 2	to foresee and provide for
PRÓXIMUS, próxima, próximum, adj.	nearest, neighbouring, related
PRUDENS, prudéntis, adj.	wise, prudent
PSALLO, psállere, psalli, —, 3	to sing to and play on a stringed instrument
PSALMUS, psalmi, m.	psalm
PSALTÉRIUM, psaltérii, n.	psaltery
PUDÍCUS, pudíca, pudícum, adj.	chaste, modest
PUDOR, pudóris, m.	1. decency, modesty. 2. shame, cause for shame
PUER, púeri, m.	boy
PUERÍLIS, pueríle, adj.	of children, child-like
PUÉRPERA, puérperae, f.	child-bearer, mother
PULCHRITÚDO, pulchritúdinis, f.	beauty
PULLUS, pulli, m.	the young of animals
PULSO, pulsáre, pulsávi, pulsátum, 1	to strike, beat, knock
PUPÍLLA, pupíllae, f.	pupil of the eye
PURGÁTIO, purgatiónis, f.	purification
PURGO, purgáre, purgávi, purgátum, 1	to cleanse, purge
PURÍFICO, purificáre, purificávi, purificátum, 1	to purify
PÚRITAS, puritátis, f.	purity
PURUS, pura, purum, adj.	pure
PUSILLÁNIMIS, pusillánime, adj.	faint-hearted
QUACÚMQUE, adv.	in whatever way
QUADRAGÍNTA, num. adj. indecl.	forty
QUAERO, quaérere, quaesívi, quaesítum, 3	to seek
QUAESO, quaésere, quaesívi, —, 3	to pray, beseech
QUÁMDIU, adv.	while, as long as
QUANDO, conj. and adv.	when
QUANTUS, quanta, quantum, adj.	how great, how much
QUANTO ... TANTO, adv.	the more ... the more
QUAPRÓPTER, conj.	on account of which
QUARE, interrog. adv.	why?

QUASI, adv.	as, thus, QUASI MODO, – in such a way
QUÁTENUS, adv.	{ 1. so that.
	2. since, as
QUATRIDUÁNUS, quatriduána, quatriduánum, adj.	of four days
QUEMÁDMODUM, adv.	as, just as
QUI, quae, quod. rel. pron.	who, which
QUIA, conj.	for, because, that
QUICÚMQUE, quaecúmque, quodcúmque, relat. pron.	whoever, everyone who, whichever, everything which
QUIÉSCO, quiéscere, quiévi, quiétum, 3	to rest, to be at peace
QUINQUE, num. adj. indecl.	five
QUÓNIAM, conj.	for, because
QUOQUE, conj.	also
QUOTÁNNIS, adv.	every year, year by year
QUÓTIES, interrog. adv.	how often?
QUOTIESCÚMQUE, adv.	as often as
QUOTQUOT, adj. indecl.	as many as
RÁDIUS, rádii, m.	ray
RAMUS, rami, m.	branch, bough
RÁPIO, rápere, rápui, raptum, 5	to seize
RATIONÁBILIS, rationábile, adj.	reasonable, rational
RATUS, rata, ratum, adj.	ratified, valid
RECÉNSEO, recensére, recénsui, recénsum (recensítum), 2	to recall, celebrate
RÉCOLO, recólere, recólui, recúltum, 3	to call to mind
RECONCILIÁTIO, reconciliatiónis, f.	reconciliation
RECONCÍLIO, reconciliáre, reconciliávi, reconciliátum, 1	to reconcile
RECORDÁTIO, recordatiónis, f.	remembrance, memory
RECÓRDOR, recordári, —, recordátus, 1	to remember
RÉCREO, recreáre, recreávi, recreátum, 1	to create anew, restore
RECTE, adv.	rightly, properly
RECTUS, recta, rectum, adj.	upright, righteous
RECÚRRO, recúrrere, recúrri, recúrsum, 3	to return, revert, recur
REDDO, réddere, réddidi, rédditum, 3	to return, give back
REDÉMPTIO, redemptiónis, f.	redemption
REDÉMPTOR, redemptóris, m.	redeemer
RÉDIMO, redímere, redémi, redémptum, 3	to redeem
REDÚNDO, redundáre, redundávi, redundátum, 1	to overflow
RÉFERO, reférre, rétuli (réttuli), relátum, irreg.	to bring, convey, announce
REFÍCIO, reficere, reféci, reféctum, 3	to restore, refresh
REFLORÉSCO, refloréscere, reflórui, —, 3	to bloom or blossom again
REFÓRMO, reformáre, reformávi, reformátum, 1	to shape again, renew
REFRIGÉRIUM, refrigérii, n.	refreshment, coolness
REFÚGIUM, refúgii, n.	refuge
REGÁLIS, regále, adj.	royal
REGENERÁTIO, regeneratiónis, f.	a being born again, rebirth
REGÉNERO, regeneráre, regenerávi, regenerátum, 1	to bring forth again, give new life to
REGNO, regnáre, regnávi, regnátum, 1	to reign
REGNUM, regni, n.	kingdom
REGO, régere, rexi, rectum, 3	to rule, govern
RELÁXO, relaxáre, relaxávi, relaxátum, 1	to loose, forgive
RELÍNQUO, relínquere, relíqui, relíctum, 3	to leave behind
RELÚCEO, relucére, relúxi, —, 2	to shine out, give light
REMÉDIUM, remédii, n.	remedy
REMINÍSCOR, reminísci, —, 3 dep.	to remember, call to mind
REMÍSSIO, remissiónis, f.	forgiveness
REMUNERÁTIO, remunerationis, f.	reward
RENÁSCOR, renásci, renátus sum, 3 dep.	to be born again
RÉNOVO, renováre, renovávi, renovátum, 1	to renew
RÉPARO, reparáre, reparávi, reparátum, 1	to restore
REPÉNTE, adv.	suddenly
REPÉRIO, reperíre, réperi (répperi), repértum, 4	to find out, find again
RÉPLEO, replére, replévi, replétum, 2	to fill

REPÓNO, repónere, repósui, repósitum, 3	to place, put back again
REPÓRTO, reportáre, reportávi, reportátum, 1	to bring back, obtain
REPRAESÉNTO, repraesentáre, repraesentávi, repraesentátum, 1	to bring before, to show
RÉPROBO, reprobáre, reprobávi, reprobátum, 1	to reject, condemn
RÉQUIES, requiéi, f. (sing. only)	rest
REQUÍRO, requírere, requisívi, requisítum, 3	to seek for, ask for
RES, rei, f.	thing, object, matter
RÉSERO, reseráre, reserávi, reserátum, 1	to open, reveal, make clear
RESPÍCIO, respícere, respéxi, respéctum, 5	to look upon
RESPÓNSUM, respónsi, n.	statement, opinion, answer
RÉSPUO, respúere, réspui, —, 3	to disapprove, not to accept
RESTAÚRO, restauráre, restaurávi, restaurátum, 1	to restore, rebuild
RESÚRGO, resúrgere, resurréxi, resurréctum, 3	to rise again
RESURRÉCTIO, resurrectiónis, f.	1. resurrection. 2. arising, getting up
RETE, retis, n.	net
RETRÍBUO, retribúere, retríbui, retribútum, 3	to give back, repay
RETRIBÚTIO, retributiónis, f.	reward, favour
RETRÓRSUM, adv.	back, backwards
REVELÁTIO, revelatiónis, f.	revelation
REVÉLO, reveláre, revelávi, revelátum, 1	to unveil, reveal
REVÍVO, revívere, —, revíctum, 3	to come to life again, revive
RÉVOCO, revocáre, revocávi, revocátum, 1	to call back
REX, regis, m.	king
RÍGIDUS, rígida, rígidum, adj.	stiff, rigid
ROBOR, róboris, n.	strength
RÓBORO, roboráre, roborávi, roborátum, 1	to strengthen
ROGO, rogáre, rogávi, rogátum, 1	to ask
RORO, roráre, rorávi, rorátum, 1	to let fall, drop, or distil dew
ROS, roris, m.	dew
ROTA, rotae, f.	wheel
RUDIMÉNTUM, rudiménti, n.	first attempt, beginning
RUÍNA, ruínae, f.	fall, destruction
SÁBAOTH (Hebrew)	'of great armies'
SACER, sacra, sacrum, adj.	holy, sacred
SACÉRDOS, sacerdótis, m.	priest
SACRAMÉNTUM, sacraménti, n.	sacrament
SACRIFÍCIUM, sacrifícii, n.	sacrifice
SACRO, sacráre, sacrávi, sacrátum, 1	to dedicate, set apart as sacred
SACROSÁNCTUS, sacrosáncta, sacrosánctum, adj.	most holy
SACRUM, sacri, n.	holy thing, place or action
SAÉCULUM, saéculi, n.	1. age, century. 2. world
SAEPE, adv.	often
SAGÍTTA, sagíttae, f.	arrow
SAL, salis, m.	salt
SÁLIO, salíre, sálui, saltum, 4	to spring up
SALÚBER or SALÚBRIS, salúbre, adj.	health-giving
SALÚBRITER, adv.	wholesomely, beneficially
SALUS, salútis, f.	health, safety, deliverance
SALUTÁRE, salutáris, n.	salvation
SALUTÁRIS, salutáre, adj.	saving, of salvation, beneficial
SALÚTIFER, salutífera, salutíferum, adj.	that brings salvation
SALVÁTOR, salvatóris, m.	saviour
SALVE (from sálveo: only this form used), 2	hail!
SALVO, salváre, salvávi, salvátum, 1	to save
SALVUS, salva, salvum, adj.	saved, safe, whole
SÁNCIO, sancíre, sanxi, sanctum, 4	to appoint as sacred, establish
SANCTIFICÁTIO, sanctificatiónis, f.	sanctification
SANCTIFICÁTOR, sanctificatóris, m.	sanctifier
SANCTÍFICO, sanctificáre, sanctificávi, sanctificátum, 1	to sanctify
SÁNCTITAS, sanctitátis, f.	holiness

SANCTUS, sancta, sanctum, adj.	holy
SANCTUS, sancti, m. ⎫	
SANCTA, sanctae, f. ⎭	saint
SANGUIS, sánguinis, m.	blood
SÁNITAS, sanitátis, f.	soundness, health
SANO, sanáre, sanávi, sanátum, 1.	to heal
SAPIÉNTER, adv.	wisely
SAPIÉNTIA, sapiéntiae, f.	wisdom
SAPOR, sapóris, m.	taste, savour
SÁTAGO, satágere, satégi, —, 3	⎰ 1. to give satisfaction ⎱ 2. to be busy
SÁTIO, satiáre, satiávi, satiátum, 1	to fill, satisfy
SATÚRITAS, saturitátis, f.	plenty, abundance
SÁTURO, saturáre, saturávi, saturátum, 1	to satisfy, provide with abundantly
SAÚCIUS, saúcia, saúcium, adj.	wounded
SCABÉLLUM, scabélli, n.	stool, footstool
SCÁNDALUM, scándali, n.	stumbling-block, cause of offence
SCÁPULAE, scapulárum, f.pl.	shoulders
SCELERÁTUS, sceleráta, scelarátum, adj.	wicked
SCEPTRUM, sceptri, n.	sceptre
SCIÉNTIA, sciéntiae, f.	knowledge
SCIO, scire, scivi, scitum, 4	to know
SCISSÚRA, scissúrae, f.	a tearing, dividing
SCRIBA, scribae, m.	scribe, writer
SCRIBO, scríbere, scripsi, scriptum, 3	to write
SCRIPTÚRA, scriptúrae, f.	scripture
SCUTUM, scuti, n.	shield
SE, sui, reflex. pron.	himself, herself, itself
SECTOR, sectári, sectátus, 1 dep.	to follow continually or eagerly
SECÚNDO, adv.	a second time
SECÚNDUM, (+acc.) prep.	according to
SECÚRUS, secúra, secúrum, adj.	safe
SECUS, adv.	by, beside, near
SED, conj.	but
SÉDEO, sedére, sedi, sessum, 2	to sit
SEDES, sedis, f.	seat, throne
SEDO, sedáre, sedávi, sedátum, 1	to assuage
SÉDULUS, sédula, sédulum, adj.	diligent, earnest
SEMEL, adv.	once
SEMEN, séminis, n.	seed, descendants
SEMETÍPSUM, emphatic reflex. pron.	himself
SÉMITA, sémitae, f.	path
SEMPER, adv.	always
SEMPITÉRNUS, sempitérna, sempitérnum, adj.	everlasting
SENÉCTUS, senectútis, f.	old age
SENÉSCO, senéscere, sénui, —, 3	to grow old
SENEX, senis, m . or f.	old man, woman
SENSUS, sensus, m.	perception, sense
SENTÉNTIA, senténtiae, f.	way of thinking, purpose
SÉNTIO, sentíre, sensi, sensum, 4	to feel, experience
SÉPARO, separáre, separávi, separátum, 1	to separate
SEPÉLIO, sepelíre, sepelívi, sepúltum, 4	to bury
SEPTENÁRIUS, septenária, septenárium, adj.	sevenfold
SEPÚLCHRUM, sepúlchri, n.	tomb, sepulchre
SEQUOR, sequi, secútus sum, 3 dep.	to follow
SERÉNUS, seréna, serénum, adj.	serene, bright
SÉRIES, (no. gen. or dat.) f.	succession
SERMO, sermónis, m.	word, speech, discourse
SERPENS, serpéntis, m. or f.	serpent
SÉRVIO, servíre, sérvii, servítum, 4	to serve
SERVÍTIUM, servítii, n.	service
SÉRVITUS, servitútis, f.	bondage, servitude

SERVO, serváre, servávi, servátum, 1	{ 1. to keep, preserve { 2. to observe, watch
SERVUS, servi, m.	servant
SÉSSIO, sessiónis, f.	act of sitting down
SEX, num. adj. indecl.	six
SI, conj.	if
SIC, adv. } SICUT, sícuti, adv. }	as, thus
SIGNÁTUS, signáta, signátum, adj.	sealed, marked
SÍGNIFER, signíferi, m.	standard-bearer
SIGNO, signáre, signávi, signátum, 1	to sign, seal, signify
SIGNUM, signi, n.	sign
SILÉNTIUM, siléntii, n.	silence
SÍLEO, silére, silui, —, 2	to be silent
SÍMILIS, símile, adj.	like, similar
SIMILITÚDO, similitúdinis f.	likeness
SIMPLEX, símplicis, adj.	simple, straightforward, honest
SIMPLÍCITAS, simplicitátis, f.	simplicity, openness
SIMUL, adv.	at the same time
SINCÉRE, adv.	sincerely
SINCÉRITAS, sinceritátis, f.	sincerity
SINCÉRUS, sincéra, sincérum, adj.	sincere
SINE (+ abl.), prep.	without
SINGULÁRIS, singuláre, adj.	unique, remarkable
SINGULÁRITAS, singularitátis, f.	oneness
SÍNGULI, síngulae, síngula, distrib. adj. (pl.)	each single one
SISTO, sístere, stiti, statum, 3	{ 1. to set up { 2. to present (a person or cause)
SITIO, sitíre, sitívi (-ii), —, 4	to be thirsty
SITIS, sitis, f.	thirst, dryness
SÓBOLES, sóbolis, f.	offspring, children
SOCIÁTIO, sociatiónis, f.	union
SOCÍETAS, societátis, f.	fellowship
SÓCIO, sociáre, sociávi, sociátum, 1	to unite
SÓCIUS, sócia, sócium, adj.	together, allied
SOL, solis, m.	sun
SOLÁTIUM, solátii, n.	comfort, solace
SOLÍDITAS, soliditátis, f.	solidity
SOLLÉMNIS, sollémne, adj.	solemn
SOLLÉMNITAS, sollemnitátis, f.	solemnity
SOLLÉMNITER, adv.	solemnly
SOLLÍCITUS, sollícita, sollícitum, adj.	stirred up, concerned about
SOLUM, adv.	only
SOLUS, sola, solum, adj. and pron.	alone, only
SOLVO, sólvere, solvi, solútum, 3	to loose, free
SOMNUS, somni, m.	sleep
SONÓRUS, sonóra, sonórum, adj.	loud, resounding
SONUS, soni, m.	sound, noise
SÓRDIDUS, sórdida, sórdidum, adj.	filthy
SOROR, soróris, f.	sister
SORS, sortis, f.	lot, part, fate. MÍTTERE SORTEM: to cast lots
SPECIÁLIS, speciále, adj.	particular, special
SPÉCIES, speciéi, f.	{ 1. outward appearance. { 2. loveliness
SPECIÓSUS, speciósa, speciósum, adj.	beautiful, fair
SPÉCULUM, spéculi, n.	mirror
SPERO, speráre, sperávi, sperátum, 1	to hope
SPES, spei, f.	hope
SPIRITALIS or SPIRITÚALIS, spiritále, adj.	spiritual
SPIRITÁLITER, or SPIRITUÁLITER, adv.	spiritually
SPÍRITUS, spíritus, m.	spirit
SPLENDOR, splendóris, m.	splendour

SPONSUS, sponsi, m.	husband, bridegroom
SPUTUM, sputi, n.	spittle
STABÍLIO, stabilíre, stabilívi, stabilítum, 4	to make firm, fix, establish
STÁBILIS, stábile, adj.	firm, steadfast, enduring
STÁDIUM, stádii, n.	course, race
STÁTUO, statúere, státui, statútum, 3	to set up, establish
STATÚRA, statúrae, f.	height, stature
STATUS, status, m.	standing, essence, substance
STELLA, stellae, f.	star
STERCUS, stércoris, n.	dunghill
STERÍLITAS, sterilitátis, f.	unfruitfulness, barrenness
STÍPULA, stípulae, f.	stubble, straw
STO, stare, steti, statum, 1	to stand
STÚDEO, studére, stúdui, —, 2	to be eager, zealous
STÚDIUM, stúdii, n.	zeal, application to learning
SUÁVIS, suáve, adj.	sweet, kind, good
SUÁVITAS, suavitátis, f.	sweetness, goodness
SUB (+abl. and acc.), prep.	under, below
SUBDO, súbdere, súbdidi, súbditum, 3	to subject, subdue
SÚBEO, subíre, subívi (-ii), súbitum, irreg.	to undergo
SUBJÍCIO, subjícere, subjéci, subjéctum, 3	to subdue, place beneath oneself
SÚBLEVO, subleváre, sublevávi, sublevátum, 1	to lift up
SUBLÍMIS, sublíme, adj.	on high
SUBMÓVEO, submovére, submóvi, submótum, 2	to remove, move off or away
SÚBSEQUOR, súbsequi, subsecútus sum, 3 dep.	to follow closely after, imitate
SUBSÍDIUM, subsídii, n.	help, aid
SUBSÍSTO, subsístere, súbstiti, súbstitum, 3	to take a position, stand still
SUBSTÁNTIA, substántiae, f.	1. substance, being. 2. property, goods
SUBVÉNIO, subveníre, subvéni, subvéntum, 4	to help
SUCCÚRRO, succúrrere, succúrri, succúrsum, 3	to aid
SUDÁRIUM, sudárii, n.	cloth, shroud
SUFFÍCIO, sufficere, sufféci, sufféctum, 5	to suffice
SUFFRÁGIUM, suffrágii, n.	support
SUM, esse, fui, —. irreg.	to be
SUMMUM, summi, n.	top, summit
SUMMUS, summa, summum, adj.	chief, highest
SUMO, súmere, sumpsi, sumptum, 3	1. to take up, consume. 2. to take on
SUPER (+ acc.), prep.	1. on, above. 2. greater, more than
SUPERLÚCROR, superlucrári, —, 1 dep.	to gain in addition
SUPÉRNUS, supérna, supérnum, adj.	heavenly, above
SÚPERO, superáre, superávi, superátum, 1	to overcome
SUPERPÓSITUS, superpósita, superpósitum, adj.	placed upon
SÚPPETO, suppétere, suppetívi, suppetítum, 3	to be present, at hand
SUPPLEX, súpplicis, adj.	humbly begging, beseeching
SUPPLICÁTIO, supplicatiónis, f.	public prayer, supplication
SUPPLÍCITER, adv.	humbly
SÚPPLICO, supplicáre, supplicávi, supplicátum, 1	to implore, pray humbly
SUPRA (+ acc.), prep.	over, above, upon
SURGO, súrgere, surréxi, surréctum, 3	to rise up
SURSUM, adv.	up, upwards
SUSCÉPTIO, susceptiónis, f.	a receiving
SUSCÉPTOR, susceptóris, m.	guardian, protector
SUSCÍPIO, suscípere, suscépi, suscéptum, 5	to take up, accept
SÚSCITO, suscitáre, suscitávi, suscitátum, 1	to raise up
SUSTÍNEO, sustinére, sustínui, susténtum, 2	to sustain, support
SUUS, sua, suum, possess. adj.	his, her, its, their

TABERNÁCULUM, tabernáculi, n.	tabernacle
TACTUS, tactus, m.	a touching, feeling
TALÉNTUM, talénti, n.	talent (piece of money)
TAM, adv.	so very, to such a high degree
TANGO, tángere, tétigi, tactum, 3	to touch

TANTUM, adv.	1. only 2. so much
TANTUS, tanta, tantum, adj.	so great
TARDO, tardáre, tardávi, tardátum, 1	to delay
TÁRTARUS, Tártari, m.	the infernal regions, hell
TAURUS, tauri, m.	bull, bullock
TECTUM, tecti, n.	roof
TEGO, tégere, texi, tectum, 3	to cover, shelter, enfold
TEGUMÉNTUM, teguménti, n.	covering, defence, protection
TEMPÉRIES, temperiéi, f.	relief, refreshment
TEMPLUM, templi, n.	temple
TEMPORÁLIS, tempórale, adj.	temporal, earthly
TEMPUS, témporis, n.	time
TENDO, téndere, teténdi, tentum (tensum), 3	1. to stretch, extend. 2. direct one's course
TÉNEBRAE, tenebrárum, f. plur. (but singular in meaning)	darkness
TÉNEO, tenére, ténui, tentum, 2	to hold, keep
TENTÁTIO, tentatiónis, f.	temptation
TÉRMINO, termináre, terminávi, terminátum, 1	to bring to an end, set bounds to
TÉRMINUS, términi, m.	limit, bound
TERRA, terrae, f.	earth, world
TERRÉNUS, terréna, terrénum, adj.	earthly
TERRÉSTER, terréstris, terréstre, adj.	earthly, on earth
TERRÍBILIS, terríbile, adj.	fearful, awesome
TÉRTIUS, tértia, tértium, adj.	third
TESTAMÉNTUM, testaménti, n.	testament
TESTIMÓNIUM, testimónii, n.	testimony
TESTIS, testis, m. or f.	witness
TESTOR, testári, testátus, 1 dep.	to bear witness, testify
THÁLAMUS, thálami, m.	bed-chamber, bride-chamber
THEMA, thématis, n.	theme
THORUS (or TORUS), thori, m.	bed, marriage-bed
THRONUS, throni, m.	throne
THUS, thuris, n.	frankincense
TÍMEO, timére, tímui, —, 2	to be afraid
TOLLO, tóllere, sústuli, sublátum, irreg.	1. to take away; 2. to lift up
TÓRCULAR, torculáris, n.	wine-press
TORMÉNTUM, torménti, n.	torment, pangs
TOTUS, tota, totum (gen. tótius), adj.	all
TRACTO, tractáre, tractávi, tractátum, 1	to manage, perform
TRADO, trádere, trádidi, tráditum, 3	to hand over, betray
TRAMES, trámitis, m.	course, path
TRANQUÍLLUS, tranquílla, tranquíllum, adj.	tranquil
TRÁNSEO, transíre, transívi, tránsitum, irreg.	to pass, cross over
TRANSFIGURÁTIO, transfiguratiónis, f.	transfiguration
TRÁNSIGO, transígere, transégi, transáctum, 3	accomplish, transact
TREMO, trémere, trémui, —, 3	to shake, tremble
TRÉPIDO, trepidáre, trepidávi, trepidátum, 1	to be confused, agitated, fearful
TRIBULÁTIO, tribulatiónis, f.	trouble, tribulation
TRÍBULO, tribuláre, tribulávi, tribulátum, 1	to oppress, afflict
TRÍBUO, tribúere, tríbui, tribútum, 3	to allot, assign, grant
TRIBUS, tribus, f.	tribe
TRÍNITAS, Trinitátis, f.	Trinity
TRISTÍTIA, tristítiae, f.	sadness, sorrow
TRIUMPHÁTOR, triumphatóris, m.	conqueror, one who triumphs
TRIÚMPHO, triumpháre, triumphávi, triumphátum, 1	to celebrate a triumph
TU, tuí, pron.	you (sing.)
TUBA, tubae, f.	trumpet
TÚEOR, tuéri, tutus sum, 2 dep.	to protect, uphold
TÚMULUS, túmuli, m.	grave, tomb
TURBA, turbae, f.	crowd
TURRIS, turris, f.	tower
TURTUR, túrturis, m.	turtle-dove
TUTAMÉNTUM, tutaménti, n.	safety, protection
TUUS, tua, tuum, possess. adj.	your (sing.)

TÝMPANUM, týmpani, n.	drum
UBER, úberis, n.	breast
UBI, adv.	when, where
UBICÚMQUE, adv.	wherever
UBÍQUE, adv.	everywhere
ULCUS, úlceris, n.	ulcer, sore
ULNA, ulnae, f.	arm
ÚLTIO, ultiónis, f.	a taking vengeance
ULTRA, adv. and prep.	further, longer, more
UNA, adv.	together
UNÁNIMIS, unánime. adj.	united, of one mind
UNDE, adv.	from where
UNGUÉNTUM, unguénti, n.	ointment, aromatic oil
ÚNGUO or UNGO, ungúere, unxi, unctum, 3	to anoint
UNICÓRNIS, unicórnis, m.	unicorn
ÚNICUS, única, únicum, adj.	alone
UNIGÉNITUS, unigénita, unigénitum, adj.	only-begotten
ÚNITAS, unitátis, f.	unity, oneness
UNIVÉRSUS, univérsi, m.	all things, heaven and earth
UNIVÉRSUS, univérsa, univérsum, adj.	all, whole; in plur. all people
UNQUAM, adv.	ever, at any time
UNUS, una, unum, gen. unius, num. adj.	one
USQUE, adv.	until, as far as
ÚSQUEQUO, interrog. adv.	how long?
UT, uti, conj.	1. so that 2. like, as 3. when
UTÉRQUE, útraque, utrúmque, pron. and adj.	both, each of two
ÚTERUS, úteri, m.	womb
UTÍLITAS, utilitátis, f.	benefit
ÚTINAM, adv.	if only
UTOR, uti, usus sum, 3. dep.	to use, make use of
UXOR, uxóris, f.	wife
VÁCILLO, vacilláre, vacillávi, vacillátum, 1	to waver, go to and fro
VALDE, adv.	very, exceedingly
VÁLEO, valére, válui, válitum, 2	to be strong, vigorous
VANUS, vana, vanum, adj.	vain, useless
VARÍETAS, varietátis, f.	changeableness, transitory nature
VÁRIO, variáre, variávi, variátum, 1	to alter, vary
VAS, vasis, n.	vassal, container
VEGETÁTIO, vegetatiónis, f.	an enlivening, quickening
VÉGETO, vegetáre, vegetávi, vegetátum, 1	to animate, invigorate
VÉHEMENS, veheméntis, adj.	violent, furious
VEHEMÉNTER, adv.	greatly, exceedingly
VEL, conj.	or
VELUT, conj.	like
VENÁTOR, venatóris, m.	hunter
VENERÁBILIS, venerábile, adj.	worthy of reverence
VÉNERO, veneráre, —, venerátum, 1 VÉNEROR, venerári, venerátus, 1 dep. }	to honour, revere
VÉNIA, véniae, f.	pardon.
VÉNIO, veníre, veni, ventum, 4	to come
VENTER, ventris, m.	{ 1.womb 2. stomach
VENTÚRUS, ventúra, ventúrum, adj.	that which is to come
VENTUS, venti, m.	wind
VERÁCITER, adv.	truly, truthfully
VERBUM, verbi, n.	word
VERE, (or VERO), adv.	truly
VÉRITAS, veritátis, f.	truth
VERMIS, vermis, m.	worm
VÉRUS, vera, verum, adj.	true

VESPERTÍNUS, vespertína, vespertínum, adj.	of evening
VESTER, vestra, vestrum, poss. adj.	your (pl.)
VESTÍGIUM, vestígii, n.	footstep
VESTIMÉNTUM, vestiménti, n.	garment, cloak
VESTIS, vestis, f.	garment
VETUS, véteris, adj.	old
VÉTUSTAS, vetustátis, f.	age, former ways, antiquity
VEXO, vexáre, vexávi, vexátum, 1	to agitate, injure, trouble
VIA, viae, f.	way
VIÁTICUM, viátici, n.	provision for a journey
VIÁTOR, viatóris, m.	traveller, wayfarer
VICÁRIUS, vicária, vicárium, adj.	delegated, substituted
VICES (no genitive), f. pi.	changes, alternation, succession
VÍCTIMA, víctimae, f.	victim
VÍDEO, vidére, vidi, visum, 2	to see
VÍGEO, vigére, —, —, 2	to thrive, flourish
VÍGILO, vigiláre, vigilávi, vigilátum, 1	to be watchful, vigilant
VINCO, víncere, vici, victum, 3	to overcome, conquer
VÍNCULUM, vínculi, n.	bond, chain
VINUM, vini, n.	wine
VIR, viri, m.	man
VIRGA, virgae, f.	branch, shoot, rod
VIRGÍNITAS, virginitátis, f.	virginity
VIRGO, vírginis, f.	virgin
VIRTUS, virtútis, f.	strength, vigour, moral excellence
VÍSCERA, víscerum, n. plur.	innermost parts
VISÍBILIS, visíbile, adj.	visible
VISIBÍLITER, adv.	visibly
VÍSIO, visiónis, f.	sight, vision
VITA, vitae, f.	life
VITÁLIS, vitále, adj.	of life, vital
VITIS, vitis, f.	vine
VÍTIUM, vítii, n.	vice
VITO, vitáre, vitávi, vitátum, 1	to avoid
VIVÍFICANS, vivificántis, (pres. partic. of vivífico)	giver of life
VIVÍFICO, vivificáre, vivificávi, vivificátum, 1	to give life to
VIVO, vívere, vixi, victum, 3	to live
VIVUS, viva, vivum, adj.	living, alive
VOCO, vocáre, vocávi, vocátum 1	to call
VOLO, voláre, volávi, volátum, 1	to fly
VOLO, velle, vólui, —, irreg.	to wish, want
VOLUNTÁRIE, adv.	of one's own free will
VOLÚNTAS, voluntátis, f.	will
VOLÚPTAS, voluptátis, f.	pleasure, delight
VOS, vestrum (vestri), pron.	you (pl.)
VOTUM, voti, n.	prayer, vow
VÓVEO, vovére, vovi, votum, 2	to vow, promise solemnly
VOX, VOCIS, f.	voice
VULTUS, vultus, m.	countenance, face

VOCABULARY OF PROPER NOUNS AND ADJECTIVES

ÁARON, m. indecl.	Aaron
ABEL, m. indecl.	Abel
ÁBRAHAM, Ábrahae, (or indecl.) m.	Abraham
AEGÝPTUS, Aegýpti, m.	Egypt
ÁGATHA, Ágathae f.	Agatha
AGNES, Agnétis, f.	Agnes
ALEXÁNDER, Alexándri, m.	Alexander
ANASTÁSIA, Anastásiae, f.	Anastasia
ANDRÉAS, Andréae, m.	Andrew
ARABS, Árabis adj.	Arabian, coming from Arabia
BÁBYLON, Babylónis, f.	Babylon
BÁRNABAS, Bárnabae, m.	Barnabas
BARTHOLOMÉUS, Bartholoméi, m.	Bartholomew
BÉNJAMIN, n. indecl.	Benjamin
BETHÁNIA, Bethániae, f.	Bethany
BÉTHLEHEM, n. indecl.	Bethlehem
CAECÍLIA, Caecíliae, f.	Cecilia
CHÉRUBIM, Hebrew pl.	the Cherubim
CHRISTUS, Christi, m.	Christ
CHRYSÓGONUS, Chrysógoni, m.	Chrysogonus
CLEMENS, Cleméntis, m.	Clement
CLETUS, Cleti, m.	Cletus
CORNÉLIUS, Cornélii, m.	Cornelius
COSMAS, Cosmae, m.	Cosmas
CYPRIÁNUS, Cypriáni, m.	Cyprian
DANIEL, Daniélis, m.	Daniel
DAVID, m. indecl.	David
ELÍSABETH, f. indecl.	Elizabeth
ELISÉUS, Eliséi, m.	Elisha
EMMÁNUEL, m. indecl.	Emmanuel
ÉPHRAIM, m. indecl.	Ephraim
FELÍCITAS, Felicitátis, f.	Felicity
GALILAÉA, Galilaéae, f.	Galilee
GALILAÉUS, -a, -um	Galilean
HEBRAÉUS, -a, -um, adj.	Hebrew
HEBRAÉI, Hebraeórum, m. pi.	the Hebrews
HERÓDES, Heródis, m.	Herod
IGNÁTIUS, Ignátii, m.	Ignatius
ÍSAAC, m. indecl.	Isaac
ÍSRAEL, m. indecl.	Israel
JACOB, m. indecl.	Jacob
JACÓBUS, Jacóbi, m.	James
JEROSÓLYMA, Jerosólymae, f. JERÚSALEM, n. indecl.	Jerusalem
JESSE, m. indecl.	Jesse
JESUS, Jesu, m. (irreg.)	Jesus
JOÁNNES, Joánnis, m.	John
JOB, m. indecl.	Job
JORDÁNUS, Jordáni, m.	the Jordan
JOSEPH, m. indecl.	Joseph
JUDAS, Judae, m.	Judas
JUDAÉI, Judaeórum, m. pi.	the Jews
LÁZARUS, Lázari, m.	Lazarus
LAURÉNTIUS, Lauréntii, m.	Laurence
LÍBANUS, Líbani, m.	Lebanon
LINUS, Lini, m.	Linus
LÚCIA, Lúciae, f.	Lucy
MANÁSSE, m. indecl.	Manasses

MARCELLÍNUS, Marcellíni, m.	Marcellinus
MARÍA, Maríae, f.	Mary
MARÍA MAGDALÉNA, Maríae Magdalénae, f.	Mary Magdalen
MATTHÉUS, Matthéi, m.	Matthew
MATTHÍAS, Matthíae, m.	Matthias
MESSÍAS, Messíae, m.	the Messiah
MELCHÍSEDECH, m. indecl.	Melchisedech
MÍCHAEL, Michaélis, m.	Michael
MÓYSES, Móysi, m.	Moses
NICODÉMUS, Nicodémi, m.	Nicodemus
ÓRIENS, Oriéntis (partic. of *orior*)	the East
PARÁCLITUS, Parácliti, m.	the Paraclete, Advocate, Comforter, Holy Spirit
PASCHA, Paschae, f. } PASCHA, Páschatis, n. }	1. the feast of the Passover. 2. Easter
PAULUS, Pauli, m.	Paul
PENTECÓSTE, -es f. (Greek)	fiftieth, the day of Pentecost
PERPÉTUA, Perpétuae, f.	Perpetua
PETRUS, Petri, m.	Peter
PHILÍPPUS, Philíppi, m.	Philip
PÓNTIUS PILÁTUS, Póntii Piláti, m.	Pontius Pilate
SABA, Sabae, f.	Seba
SÁBAOTH, Hebrew f. pl.	'great armies'
SAMARITÁNA, Samaritánae, f.	Samaritan woman
SÁMUEL, Samuélis, m.	Samuel
SÁTANAS, Sátanae (or SATAN indecl.), m.	Satan
SÍMEON, Simeónis, m.	Simeon
SIMON, Simónis, m.	Simon
SINA, f. indecl.	Sinai
SION, m. f. or n. indecl.	Sion
THADDAÉUS, Thaddaéi, m.	Thaddeus
THARSIS, m. or f. indecl.	Tarshish
XYSTUS, Xysti, m.	Sixtus
ZACHARÍAS, Zacharíae, m.	Zacharias, Zachary